HOW THE HELL DID
WE GET HERE?

HOW THE HELL DID WE GET HERE?

Wini Mgidi

Library of Congress Control Number:		2013900248
ISBN:	Hardcover	978-1-4797-7532-3
	Softcover	978-1-4797-7531-6
	Ebook	978-1-4797-7533-0

This book was printed in the United States of America.

To order additional copies of this book, contact:
Xlibris Corporation
0-800-644-6988
www.xlibrispublishing.co.uk
orders@xlibrispublishing.co.uk
305449

Contents

Dedication

As iron sharpens iron, so one person sharpens another.

(Prov. 27: 17)

This book is dedicated to those who dare to pursue love in the midst and absence of their gut. For love is a race worth running, a pain worth feeling, and victory in every way.

Acknowledgements

A fool's mouth lashes out with pride, but the lips of the wise protect them.

(Prov. 14: 3)

God my strength.

Grandmother and late grandfather: you raised a heroine.

Mom and Dad: there was method in your strict rules.

Kingdom Ngwenya: wishing you blessings untold for being my spiritual mentor.

Xhirandziwa: my daughter, the *beloved one*, know that you can do all things through him who strengthens you.

Simphiwe, Samu, and Deborah: my sisters, please surround yourselves with positive people, and remember, the fear of the *Lord* is the beginning of wisdom.

Liefling: thank you for loving me unconditionally.

Critics: keep doing it. I love it! You inspire me!

Racists: I know you are out there. Your days are numbered.

My precious readers: thank you for picking this one up. To those who dare to take this journey with us . . . reach out for the top of the mountain.

Preface: Just a Thought

Above all else, guard your heart, for everything you do flows from it.

(Prov. 4: 23)

I thought I loved him. That's about as close to the truth as it gets. It was not a definite conviction or the lack thereof. It was not one of those stories whereby I *knew* from the word go that this is *it*. Something lingered in my gut that I just could not shake off. Something whispered in the atmosphere that I just could not pinpoint.

I don't know how to describe it. It would be like describing a cloud in the atmosphere. It is there, and you know it. It hovers and lurks around. It has a presence, but no heartbeat. Sometimes you want to catch it, but it is out of reach. Other times you want to grab it and embrace it, but it is just vapour, a little gas which is disguised.

Just when you give up on its existence, hail and rain reassure you that it is there. It cannot be ignored nor sidetracked. The cloud is there and starts controlling your temperature. It gives you goosebumps and makes you shiver. Even though it is out *there*, it controls what is in here.

And so, my humble thought was not just something outside of myself but in me. It was real. I really thought I loved him. Could it be that I was the only one that was struggling with the recognition of love? Was I the only one chasing after a deeper level of intimacy that persisted after the butterflies were gone?

Did other brides-to-be *know* that they were indeed in love? When one considers the perfect, flawless face and fairy-tale wedding, it is hard to pinpoint that there is a flicker of doubt. Yet, I have asked myself over and over if this is the exception. The more I interact with others on a personal level, the more human I start to feel.

I start getting the feeling that in as much as I thought I was the exception for not knowing for sure that I loved him with every fibre of my being; something within me did love him and another did not.

I was not forced into cohesion. There was no gun pointed to my head or an external pressure that coined me to get involved in the first place. Just me and that little voice inside that asked, 'What on earth are you doing?'

I think I needed him to complete the picture in my head that I had drafted out as a little girl. I had what I call *the list*. I needed to tick off some things and he was there at the right time and place.

He was my knight in shining armour. He was that which I had made up since my childish dreams and fantasies. He was the fantasy personified. A valiant prince. Nothing less than a vision. A pleasure to behold. A sparkle.

He was the vehicle for me to access a deeper level of intimacy than I have ever done on my own. I think my heart was set at the right place, or what I thought was the right place in that moment in time. It was like competing with myself for myself.

In him, I could access the fairy tale I had crafted with my childhood ambitions. He was my channel to being a wife and mother. Without him, there was no perfect family portrait. It would have seemed incomplete and unthinkable. Without him, I was complete; I just did not know it at the time.

All I vividly remember was me not being able to answer the question of whether I loved him other than I *think* I did. I never voiced it out in public, but I asked myself that question over and over.

As the idea of getting married marinated within me, I just could not shake the idea that I was not sold over somewhere deep down. I looked like I was, but then again, I was not.

There was no engrafted conviction. I cared for him as best as I could. I adored him and respected him as my husband-to-be. I wanted to take care of him as best as I could.

I had a reverence for him as the father of my child. He was no longer an individual, but someone that was deeply entrenched into me. I enacted the perfect wife-to-be from having been in this moment over and over in my mind.

I portrayed the perfect illustrations. It was the show of my life, and I was the leading lady. This was not a show that just started, but something that had been going on for a long while.

I think, in all earnestness, we knew that we were patching up cracks even before we got married, but what the heck, we were young and the world was my oyster. The moment was now, and we had the energy and charm of youth to seal it.

In me, he would unleash his endeavours as a father and husband. With me, he would be himself and have another one that looked a lot like him. Together, we would multiply and then form one more.

In me, the image of a family arose. It was no longer an idea or a thought that we both wanted to bring to life; it was a reality that was now closer than ever before. We both wanted the same thing in this regard.

Our individual selves took a bash when we decided to marry. They looked and were found lacking. They would be forever displaced. Dead and buried. No longer would I be who I was. I wanted to be new. I wanted to be transformed. I looked forward to it.

Did he love me?

As in, did he truly love me? Only he knows the answer to that. I am not going to pretend to be a bogus mind reader or speak on behalf of another. I can just say that actions spoke for themselves.

The answers resided within individuals. Only the human hearts that were entwined could individually answer that question. It is not something that sought to be jotted down and marketed to the world, but something that needed to be known by those involved.

I thought that my new family was nothing less than my everything. They were my very life. Even while enacting the notions and perfect bliss, all I told myself was I had to tick this off my list and then I would be happy. Happiness was not the process but the end result.

Before this, happiness was graduating top of my class while at tertiary. I was not happy while I had sleepless nights and others partied the night away. I was not happy to bleed and tear up for the sake of reading one more page. I stretched myself to extortion.

I beat my will until it was broken beyond recognition. I forced my eyes to stay awake and bruised my mind to study when it could not take in anything any more. When my body collapsed out of exhaustion, I militated against it and forced it to go further. I had a goal, and it cost me much to tick it off.

I am a professional. I don't hold my heart on my sleeve. You will never see me fall apart. I work hard in all that I do. I work even harder when something is hurting me deep down in my soul, and I do not know how to fix it.

It was not intuitive that I came out tops. The process was not fun, but I had a goal. My goal was to give it my all and to press for gold. I obtained gold. Like an athlete, I often bled. I felt the pressure and had hurdles of discouragement to overcome.

It was not easy, it was often very hard. Yet I pressed on for the golden prize. I fainted along the way but resuscitated myself in moments when there was no one else to help me out. When there was no study buddy or money for a private tutor, I encouraged myself. I ministered to myself.

Sometimes you need to encourage yourself and rip open your own heart, squeeze it, pump it, and breathe into it in order to save it. It pains like crazy. It feels like an overwhelming hurricane at times. Yet, in life, we often need hurricanes to blow away the fluffs that we think we cannot live without.

When my name was called out and I obtained my goal of leading the pack, it was all worth it. I ticked it off and smiled. Very few people, if any, knew the sacrifice it took to come out on top. Some even brushed it off on notions that I have good genes. I just smiled and ticked it off as a goal accomplished. I ticked it off and focussed on the next tick.

Marriage was one of those things that was next on my list. Love was another I longed to embrace and contain in my space as I ticked it. In order to obtain the tick, I had to sacrifice a lot.

At times the sacrifice was no longer out there, but within myself. I had to give up *me* for the sake of ticking off my fairy-tale wedding. Here was a man and there I was, ready and looking forward to ticking off.

In order to get to the baby, we needed to join together various elements. We needed to strip to a level of deepest intimacy. We needed to be alone behind closed doors and there, be known to each other.

There was a need for blood and gut. Several wonderful and painful encounters. The overarching goal was more important than the actual journey. It was and has been worth every mile.

At times, once you have compromised all you can, you can no longer compromise. Once you have stretched and stretched, you can't do so any more. You begin to tear. You start ripping from the inside. It is not long until the damage takes its toll. The stitches come undone. An unwinding begins and you dismember.

The pain takes its toll. Wear and tear kicks in. It is now more than ever before that you had better have a clear goal of why you are doing this. It is now that you ask questions that you never knew existed.

This dismembering is part of the process to reach the set targets. When compromise reaches its highest peak, you are faced with the option of giving up or taking it to the next level.

This is when operation sacrifice kicks in. You start throwing out what you love and want in order to keep the boat afloat. You recognise that this is a sinking ship and therefore start throwing out mediocre and prized possessions in order to get to the other side.

You are confronted with abandoning the ship and its wreckages or learning to walk on water. If ever you needed a miracle, it is now. You walk for as long as you can and try everything out of desperation.

You swallow as much water as you can. You take in sea water and swallow it even though you know it is not good for you. You walk on water. Swim on land. Walk on hot coals without a splinter.

Even while going through this storm, you know that you must not bleed. You must not bleed or else you may attract sharks at your most vulnerable point. This is not the time to show any emotion or to entertain the fear that is bubbling up within you.

And so I learnt to put on a happy face. Amidst the trials and joys. I put on a happy face and was seemingly the happiest girlfriend, happiest bride-to-be, happiest wife, happiest mom . . . happiest me.

Tick.

One can only cover up so much until the wardrobe door bursts open and things spill out that cannot be contained. There is only so much that can be done to prevent the door from exposing the secrets within.

One can only bandage and plaster a septic wound so much until greenish-yellow puss oozes out and a stench emerges from the wound gasping for air and attention in order to be cleaned.

I tried.

No one wants to have their closet burst open and the mess hidden inside fall apart. However, knowing what I now know, I think it is safe to say that sometimes we need to fall apart in order to mend again. Sometimes we need the situation to reach dangerous limits and plateau beyond our mere forecasts.

We need the wind to blow off our roofs and rattle our homesteads so that we can know where *home* is. For the real home cannot be altered. It is not moved by a mere location or geographical divide.

In order to locate home, we often need to be lost beyond measure. Lost to the extent that we know we cannot find our way anywhere else than that innate compass within, redirecting us back home.

Home cannot be far, for it is where our inner, whole, and complete self resides. We lose that when we are far from home. We regain that when we are naked and blatantly honest with none other than self.

My marriage did not survive. That was not part of the tick. That was not part of the plan. I don't think anyone goes in for the sake of going in to pan the land. We go in full of only the best of hopes.

You don't marry for the sake of ticking and celebrating, and I did that. Even though the odds are high and statistics quiver, one does not make marriage vows and back up plans just in case it lasts.

I ticked.

And unticked.

I am however most grateful for our baby girl. That I cannot and will never untick. She is none other than my life. My very heartbeat. The best part of both of us. Totally all that and more.

She resembles the me I was before the list emerged. I see him in her. I see the best of him and am reminded why we got together in the first place. In her, I am. She is testament to the productivity in me. She is just downright beautiful to me.

When the urge to draw up more lists comes and goes, I just look at her, and I am persuaded that it does not get better than this. I am comforted. Life finds meaning when I look at her.

Her Tsonga name 'Xirhandziwa' means 'the beloved one'. I could go on and on about her, but if you were to press me to conclude, I would simply say that she is my beloved daughter. She is to me what sun is to sky. She is like what stars and moon are to a dark sky. She lights up my world. Not only does she act as a catalyst that brings me light, but she is my world.

She is the source and centre, the heartbeat and blood, everything a mom could ever dream of. There is nothing that I would not do to protect and love her.

No matter how tempted I am to rewind and fast-forward in the lapses of time, this is the one outcome that just makes everything worthwhile. I look at her, and my entire life has meaning and accounts for a life well spent for birthing my little beloved.

As time lapses and the urge consumes me to make more tick boxes, I catch myself scurrying for paper, unwrapping crunched-up pieces of paper that I have compiled . . . I merely remind myself of her and the trembles dissipate.

Sometimes the quiver returns shortly after and other times it leaves until an opportune time, but whatever the case, I know that I have to live. I have a reason to rise even when I fall. She is my reason to dust myself off, take off, and soar.

When I start bruising myself and restraining my conscious and subconscious to get to a goal, even then I am not afraid. When I am a little scared, I don't slow down. Instead, I do it, afraid. I strengthen my knees and fortify the quivers so that I can proceed on the journey.

As I reflect, a little tingle in me asks me, 'What on earth are you doing?' I remember the tingle. I have had it before. It was there when I was afraid of moving from my humble village to go and study in the 'big city'. It was there when I was timid and made a decision in my timidity to be the very best I could be.

The tingle returned when we took leave to conceive our baby at the ideal date and time. It was there when I gave birth and I held my baby in my arms. It was there when I said 'I do'. I vividly recall it being there when we separated, and I signed the divorce papers.

Even while I mourned for the love I thought I knew and the reality I had that is no longer proving to be true, the question resurfaced, 'What on earth am I doing?' Now it comes as just a thought. I cannot deny its existence. That being said, I cannot deny my existence because of that thought.

Do it even though you are afraid, I tell myself. Even though it was part of my strongest and weakest moments, I cannot be afraid of being afraid. Even when I am, I have resolved to do it anyway, very afraid. In spite of the scariness conjuring up in my mind, the movement is set in a forward direction. There's no turning back.

I am at the verge of giving birth to the idea of another tick. I am in labour to manifest my dreams. In giving birth to this idea, I cannot stop pushing. I am at that point where stopping now would not only sabotage my dream but my very own purpose.

I am at the point of no return. I have moved way past conception and watching that which was stored up within me take form. I am now in the birthing room. It is not a pleasant place to be in.

It is for those who are not afraid to get messy and torn apart. In here, the goal is not to look together but to fall apart for the sake of giving birth to the divinity within you. The goal now is to do whatever it takes to protect the dreams the dreamer, and the vision and its carrier.

Once the labour has begun, you push. You cannot decide how much pain you can tolerate and how much you can't. It is no longer optional. You don't decide what you want to accept and can't accept. It is often a messy process, but one that is worth it.

I am in labour. There's no other way of putting it. I am in the process of pursuing the dreams that I sacrificed in order to obtain one more tick on the to-do of life. I am in the process of revising the realities that I think I know and redefining all that matters to me.

I am in the process of letting go of holding on, pulling down my hair and soaking in the sunshine. Years have passed since I was embraced, and I am now in the process of pursuing love again.

It is not an overnight sensation but a gradual process of navigating in this new territory. It feels new and yet it feels like I have been here before. I am trying again even though I know that I just didn't make it the last time.

This time, it feels different because I need to look out not only for myself but for my baby as well. I need to do all I can to protect her. Let it be known that according to statistics, the odds are against me in that it does not get 'easier' second time round.

It is not like a test that you take and fail and come back more prepared. Perhaps the contrary is true because you buckle in a bit. You return to the battle ring with bruises, battered outlooks, and the deep longing to be loved for who you are.

The little twist—that I really did not think would be a factor at all in this 'new South Africa', Post-1994 era and so-called Rainbow Nation—is that he is of a different race.

Let's just say I am attempting to navigate being a mother, daughter, career woman, and simply a human being in a relationship with a wonderful, caring, and gentle man of another race.

All this is proving to be a challenge which in itself deserves a tick. It is something that should have been straightforward and normal, but for some reason, it is not. It is to us but not so to a couple of people around us.

It was not part of the plan simply because I did not think that my heart was capable of beating fast again when in the presence of another. It is a mystery to me how I could feel affection and a warm comfort reside in me when in the vicinity of another born of a woman.

This time, I don't even wait for the tingle to emerge; I myself have taken over the tingle and sometimes find myself asking, 'What on earth am I doing?' I ask myself that for no reason at all.

I almost feel guilty for feeling this happy.

Come with me as I journey on unmarked ground. I guess it is true that you don't just fall for the individual, but their past, present, and who they will be. You take on the very confident sides and the timid part of them that does not want to break again.

You embrace a warrior woman who is a rock in every way as well as the fragile little girl within her, hoping that you won't do her wrong. When you fall in love, you don't pick aspects that suit you best, you receive the entire package.

Why is it that most women who are in relationships pretend they know exactly what they are doing? It is as though all the pieces of the puzzle are there on the table, waiting to fit perfectly together to form a delightful image.

How many times can you find 'Mr Right'? With each one that serenades the inner chords of our hearts, we pretend to be happy. Each one is supposedly the soulmate that was anticipated since the beginning of time.

How many soulmates can one have? How many times does one fall in love throughout their lifetime? How many 'I love you, my dear' are permitted to raise the eyebrow and say, 'I am happy in this moment, but I don't know where this will go.'

I know I would like it to be this way, but I won't pretend it is magical. I am not saying this because I don't believe. I am saying this because I know that the magic you see on socially constructed films is deceptive. It vanishes like smoke. It is an illusion.

Well, that's the stuff you read in the novels. This, on the contrary, is real life. The end is not neatly packed and written out. What I do know is that there is a new love in my life. He looks a little different and boy, oh boy, are we getting the heat for caring for each other.

I think the very first obstacle is fighting to be together. It is a fight. A battle. Don't be deceived: race is still a big issue here in South Africa! The discussions concerning race should not be shut as yet. In fact, they should be magnified and given a platform.

We are not only fighting our internal battles as a young couple navigating on unknown territory when we are both not as young, as young can be, but are faced with external outcries.

How about the notion that even though I know that I love him, I still don't know if this is indeed *love*. I have no idea if my boyfriend will be my knight in shining armour for as long as we both shall live.

I do know that there is tenderness in my heart for him. I can reassure you that he makes me smile even when I have had the worst of days. It is easy for me to say that, which I know, he means a lot to me right now.

This is an ongoing journey. There is no clearly marked destination or pit stop, distinguished map of where it is that you want to go. The pit stops are not all clearly marked.

I don't know how the end will unfold or if there is an end at all. Perhaps I may just discover this true love mystery, or maybe I will know that which I have always known. That love resides within and is not a farfetched concept that is out *there*.

Maybe I may just write a follow-up book telling you of the 'happily ever after', with Milkybar—and chocolate-coloured angels adding to my existing angel, sitting in the porch with my hubby next to my wrinkled arm. Or I may get hurt again, split my pencil into two, and never write another word about this journey.

I just don't want my heart to grow callous again. I don't want thorns to find a home and spread inside of me to the extent that I need to consume all of me with fire to kill the weeds and thistles.

I want to be able to continue to feel something. Whether it is love or pain, bliss or despair, I want to be able to feel as humans do. It is not my wish to always retain my composure but also my humanity. I wish to be humane and remain humane.

All things said and done, I want my little girl to know that I love her and consider her in all that I do. One day, years from now when she is older and has renewed understanding, I hope that she never doubts the magnitude of love that her mother has for her.

I don't want her to be persuaded by words but by deeds. By a conviction that stems from profound knowledge. I want her to know that she is and will always be my little girl.

I hope that in hearing my story, other stories will be given a voice. Dare not think that this is the story of everyone or that I am not cognisant of the racial unity that is evident in our nation. I really do notice and appreciate it more than words can describe.

The fact that my boyfriend is of another race and culture reinforces the miles and leaps that we have made as a nation. We have never been arrested, and I am writing this as a free woman; something which would not have been the case two decades ago!

Mzansi (South Africa) has indeed come a long way. I see it in the way my daughter interacts with her peers at school. I see it when we go to shopping malls and a stranger you have never met does a kind gesture.

The fact that I am even able to talk about my experience without fear or prejudice is a good thing that is definitely worth mentioning again. I do not take it lightly. So I am very grateful and aware that we have taken on racial challenges in leaps and bounds.

I am in no way making my story the story of everyone. It is not South Africa's story and should in no way be positioned as such. It is merely a South African's story. The story of one, which is actually not a story at all.

It is a journey. An experience and a lesson. A series of ticks and unticks. An amalgamation of smiles and tears of all my life. It is a book that in all sense is not a book at all.

Maybe it is some sort of personal journal that is not open to the world but is available to other individuals who want to pick it up and turn the pages. It is not an open invitation but something that is open for others to engage in.

In finding it, may you find a piece of yourself that dares to dream again. May you find the courage to not only sprint ahead but also to go back to the point of disaster and rectify and heal that which is covered deep down. Visit the trauma and heal the pain. Pop the blisters in your psyche.

As I say this, I think of 'the lists' and wonder how I am going to get delivered from them. I hope in these little horrors and blessings that I have coined, I can find myself, even though I know exactly where I am.

Will I ever be free from the list? Will the list transform into me? I am tackling a lifelong dilemma right here and now.

'The list' is next on my list!

The List

Plan carefully what you do, and whatever you do will turn out right.

(Prov. 4: 26)

I don't know where this madness of 'the list' started. Perhaps it is something within me that I just inherited without even knowing. All I know is that ever since I can recall, I have been collecting scraps of paper and files to put together 'the list'.

The list comprises of the landmarks in my life. The stuff I really want to achieve, places I want to see, people I want to meet, and so forth. The list is the one that dictated when I would marry and have a baby. That in turn led to decide when was the most fertile day to have a baby and the rest as they say is history.

The list jotted down my career aspirations, divine appointments, and more madness than you have ever imagined. As the years went by, I have come to justify my list with the comfort that almost everyone has some form of list in one way or another.

To be frank, I have ticked off a lot of the things that were in the original list. Yes, there is an original list that was transcribed from the mental one to one that is being modified on a continuous or need-be basis. Additions and alterations can come to me while I drive or after a profound conversation with someone, and then I do *number-two list.*

I guess this book is part of the list. I am not sure when it emerged, but it is a form of letting out the expressive me that was consumed by the rigid corporate sector. I once had an expressive voice. I think it is still there, but it is a little numb. It is faint and subdued, no longer as loud and free as it used to be.

As a young voice-over character at a popular community radio station, I had that voice, and it was heard. It was not hidden and restricted to my little room, but it shone and was heard far and wide.

I was expressive in my native language: a tongue that is close to my heart and unrestrained expression. I understood the part of my inner self that wanted to speak and be heard.

I think I lost that voice with the passing of time and the sacrifice of the creative me in order to conform. Rather than pursuing the *art*, I went for the safer route. Rather than brave it, I took on a less risky career with some sort of security.

Fortunately, the list system ensured that I would work very hard at whatever I set my mind to do. The list system was not linked to any discipline but to every aspect of my life. The list forced me to work very hard.

I worked hard and enjoyed it. I guess the creative part of me is like that analogy of the closet bursting open and messing up the neat composure. It screams along with what I have come to call the *tingle* and asks, 'What on earth are you doing?'

It refuses to be discarded and boxed for good. It is the part of me that was not accommodated by the list and is now forcing me to acknowledge it as an extension of me. It longs to conform and be accepted.

It is not the me I want to be, it is me. The only difference is that the lens has tilted and is portraying another perspective. The view seems different because the angle is not as it used to be.

A lot of my achievements can be attributed to the list.

I was once summoned for my first permanent job interview, the place was far away and I was young and inexperienced. Naïve, to say the least.

I slept very excited, but awoke despondent. I did not have the required experience. I had the qualification, drive, and personal attributes. Even though I had most of the requirements, other than the experience, I was discouraged.

My mom came to me in the very early hours of the morning, while it was still dark, and woke me up. The anxiety of how I would get there and the fear of rejection caused my timid heart to stumble. Resolute that it would not work out, I continued to sleep.

It is not as though I was sleepy. I was just scared. Why would anyone want to hire me? I was not competing with my peers or my class or my institution, I was in another league. This was real life rolling out, and I did not think I measured up.

My mom came again and found me sleeping. She pressed me to try. Even offered me her car to use while I embarked on my very first trip that spanned over four hours to Nelspruit. Just the very act of driving alone was enough to make me buckle down.

Yet, it was part of the list. The list dictated that I press on and now start working and earn a higher income. This would entail facing my fears and conquering the giants within me that constantly lied to me and said I did not measure up.

There were no more giants but myself. It was me against me. My mom pressed on. Resilient and undeterred, she spoke sense into me. Reassured me that I would not have been called and shortlisted if they did not see potential in me.

She pressed me to press myself. I heard the voice within me in spite of the fear. As she spoke, my inner core listened.

I heard her and I heard myself speaking back against the tingle. There was an inner awakening. All particles that can be constituted as *noise* were removed. Lights were dimmed and the real spotlight shone.

I heard something that I have never heard before. I heard a *me* that I knew not existed. A conversation emerged in my psyche and dared me to talk back without words.

I think it was during the first two minutes of my drive to the interview that I asked myself, 'What on earth am I doing?' I replaced the tingle with myself. I asked and a tingle arose.

It was crazy. What was I going to say when I got there? Would I even be able to drive there in one piece and return? Would my new driving skills hold out when fatigue and fear kicked in? There were more questions than answers.

The list was the little solid anchor point. It reassured me that I was doing just fine and that even though I felt like a fish outside water, I was right where I needed to be.

At times, I wanted to turn on the hazards and warning lights within my very being, turn back, and stop the madness, but the list refused. The list awoke something powerful within me that wanted to try. Something that wanted to make it in spite of all the fear.

It longed to be ticked and would not allow the insecurities within me to dampen it. Just when I thought I was in over my head and there was no way this would work out in my favour, the list dared to press on.

It reminded me of the feeling of accomplishment and reassured me that this was more about conquering self than the job itself. I had to try. I could not turn back now. This was the point of no return.

Now was my chance to bring my mind under subjection. This was an opportunity to shine. I have come to the conviction that you cannot shine unless you are in a dark space.

It is the darkness that makes light even so much more glorious. You need the darkness to awaken the light within. Darkness is better than dimmed lights. Dimmed lights give you a false sense of vision.

I needed the light, but in that moment in time, I needed the darkness to remind me that I was more lost than I had ever been. I needed utter darkness to propel me to search for the light and switch it on.

The very crazy act of going was a means of turning on the light. In order to be, I had to keep on the light. Reaching out for the light meant departing from fear. It meant acknowledging that I was timid.

I was more timid than I initially thought. Petrified. Yes, I was scared of even getting out of the yard. Worried from the word *go*. I had to remind myself which side was the indicator and struggled with the very basics.

I was not half as experienced as I should have ideally been. Yet, as my mom reassured me, I was invited for the interview. It did not matter how much I belittled myself, the reality was that those people thought there was something in me worth seeing.

At first, I reached out to them and now they were reaching out to me. People don't often get second chances and so I was not going to let mine go. This was not the time to succumb to inferiority. Not now!

This was the time to act. If ever I needed to brace myself and run, this was it. If ever I needed to do it even though I was afraid, it was now. Now was my moment, not yesterday and not tomorrow.

After many moons and a lot in between, I received the news that I got the job and a confirmation that the job was in Tzaneen. Tick. I was over the moon. I wished I wrote down the events that would unfold. I did not know then what I now know.

The tick stopped at me getting the job. It did not specify how I would handle the departure that came with getting the job. Now, once again, I had to face the fears within me. I don't know if I am the only one with the tingle or if everyone has that inner consciousness that is leaning towards unbelief. It is the realist in me. A little flicker, I cannot put my finger on.

'What on earth are you doing?'

I asked myself those questions more times than I can count. Why did I accept a job so far away? My life was here. Everything I knew, I knew from this place. Could I stand on foreign ground? How would I rate among strangers? Where was I going?

Was I going to sacrifice my life as I knew it for independence and the chance to make my own money? Was this going to be all that I thought it would be? Was I ready for this?

Before I knew it, I was in the adventure of my life. I was practically living in a suitcase and relocating once too often. I was neither here nor there. I was floating. Like clouds. I was there, but not really there. I was in this province and the next.

I was soon promoted. Tick. Promoted again. Tick. And again. Tick. Tick. It was as though I was on top of the world. I did not really know my bearings because I was goal driven. I wanted to tick continuously. I sacrificed myself in the process.

I was pruning myself to produce more and more fruit. Relocating myself to self-made greenhouses to speed up production. I beat my body to a pulp. I ripped my mind and scared it to obey. I was on cruise control. Somewhat depersonalised.

I did not really have time for emotion. I considered it to be some form of weakness. I was after goals, not feelings. This continued to sieve out my personal relations that were already a little tense.

I think I come across as somewhat cold because I aim for a goal and go for it without reservations. I am not the type strangers warm up to and start making all sort of unfounded declarations.

There is not much time to reflect and go back and forth when it comes to feelings. I am not driven by feelings. Instead, I will let them channel me to work harder to pursue my goals. I realign the passions within me.

Whereas feelings can be seen as obstacles whereby the soul comes into combat with the mind, I use feelings to press on towards the goal. I use my feelings to propel me to new dispensations.

I control and master my feelings. I do not let them roam around and do as they please. I am the boss. There are times when feelings get the best of me, but generally I do not go around with my heart on my sleeve.

I am not an open book, not even to myself. I think there are things that I hide away even from myself. I pack them so deeply that I struggle to get them out. They are there, but I hide the password to retrieve them. I hide it even from myself.

When feelings take on my mind, I allow them to roam around freely. I let them come out of the closet and flap as they please. Yet, I do this within a restricted space. I give them structured space and a designated time.

I don't just let them dominate. Best of all, I never empower them to be the deciding factor. I feel, but at the right place and time. I feel appropriately. I feel accordingly. Perhaps that's just my interpretation and self-diagnosis of emotional intelligence.

My daughter has challenged that line of thought and demolished every theory that I thought I had. At some point, I was writing a list for her and her forecasted development. I chased it and put pressure on her to comply for a while.

Yet, as I saw her pursuing *my* goals for *her*, I repented. I don't care what she does so long as she is really happy. I don't want her to live the life that I wanted to live now that I have the advantage of hindsight; I just want her to be happy.

I want her to mature at her own pace. She does not need to do anything to impress me. She already does, in every way. In being, I am. As she inhales, I exhale. When she opens her eyes, I see.

I see her in her ballerina outfit, twirling and dancing as little girls should. That makes me smile. I wave within my chambers and applaud that at least I have done something right.

I want her to play. I watch her coming to meetings with her favourite doll and I smile. I sneak a peek at her when she is not watching and my soul rejoices when I catch her brushing the doll's messed up curly hair or dressing it in various outfits.

I have resolved not to be the type of mom that only celebrates when she is at the top of her class. I am content. I never want her to stop trying. I never want her to stop pressing on and going for gold.

Better still, I never stop enforcing the fact that she already is that gold that she seeks. That at the end of her search and quest for meaning and doing this and that, I want her to find self and be content.

As she knows herself a little more, as she perfects her space and navigates through unknowns, it is important for me that she feels safe. I want her to know that she is already perfect. Perfection is not out there but a substance of who she is.

It is a fundamental truth that I actively drill within her to brainwash her as best as I can. I want her to know that mommy loves her for who she is. She does not *become* perfect; she simply *is* divine.

Yes, there are human limitations, but I want her to grow up knowing she can be anything because she *is*. I don't want her to believe me. I want her to believe in herself and know that she is unique.

I want her to believe in herself. That even if my speech and that of others can change, she will not move in her solid convictions. Yes, I want a lot of good things for my daughter. I think every parent rightfully seeks the best for her loved one.

I need her to be able to wake up in the middle of any night—be it a well lit night or a stormy escapade—and find comfort in the conviction that she is perfectly made in the image of God.

When it comes to my daughter, the list has no effect. I don't want to raise the *perfect* child. I want to foster an environment wherein my child can be nurtured into accepting and loving who she is.

All I desperately want is for her to be happy. I have no desire to shield her from living her own life. I just want her to be happy. While she is entrusted to me, I need to be there for her.

I was mainly raised by my grandmother. My mom did the best that she could under the circumstances, but my grandmother was the superstar that bent over to accommodate us.

She allowed my mom to go sort out her life and go to college and work with the reassurance that I was in good hands. Even in her old age, she raised a young child as best as she could.

As a little village girl in Weltevrede, the list was forming. It was packing up and gaining momentum. By the age of fourteen, I was working as a voice-over radio artist and I knew I was destined for great things.

Something in me refused to waver, even when surrounded by a non-conducive surrounding. There has always been a believer in me. When I need a cheer, the believer arises and serves as a witness. The believer believes.

I can't exactly tell you when, but I recall writing down what I wanted to do with my life. I knew that there was more that awaited this Mabusabesala High School pupil. My desire has never been to put Mpumalanga Province on the map. It was simply to live. To love. To be me and comfy in my own skin. To chase my goals.

The list was never part of the plan. It just came very naturally to me. One day, I found myself in deep thought and scribbling on paper. It just happened. I caught myself already having the scribbled list. By the time I came to consciousness, the list was already there.

Perhaps one day I might have a list of the list or summarise the purpose of the list in one bullet point. I have not yet come to that dispensation and will just have to do with the little lists coming together and being adjusted to form the list.

Maybe next time the list item will transcend past the encounter or meeting the man I choose to spend the rest of my life with. Perhaps the list will incorporate emotions and position emotional intelligence as the strength that it is. Who knows, my list might be consumed by my gut.

Until then, the little scribbles will continue. Until I am convinced of some form of structuring my life in a manner that allows for more flexibility, I will continue mind mapping life. I saw my grandfather do that. He was very orderly. He also went out of his way to love me.

Now that I think about it, I think my mom also has this list phenomenon. She is orderly and detailed. She can tell you where she will be in a decade to come. Perhaps not as detailed, but she is not a drifter.

She is not one to let things happen to her without adding to the mix. Not only does she contribute to the happenings in her life, she initiates the responses that she desires. Whereas people react, she is proactive.

Even when she messes up, I see her pull herself together. I see her get up and try again. I see her put on a brave face and camouflage the carved-in knees. I know that she is out of her comfort zone, but that does not cause her to tremble.

She fears, but fears being afraid even more. There were times when she repaired brokenness. I did not think that it was possible, but she did. It is something I do not know how to explain.

Sometimes it seemed like a joke when she commenced. You would have been justified for thinking that it was just a silly idea that was not going to end up anywhere. It was like scooping up a puddle with a spoon. She began scooping.

She scooped it up and continued to do so. It was ridiculous to watch. Day in and day out, she would sit by the mess of puddle proportions and do her part at restoration.

In her, I learnt that it is not just about building; you have to stop and repair. You need to come to a point whereby you reflect and fix. In life, there is a lot of wear and tear. People grind down. Courage breaks. Hopes fade.

Knowing what I now know, I will definitely put in much more room for exhaling, catching my breath, and reflecting on the list. I will put in periods of tranquillity. Rest and more rest to avoid burnout.

I also hope to know when I don't know. I wish to reach more moments of silence than conjuring up answers. Ask more questions without the pressure of needing to answer each one intellectually.

I don't want to toil. Perhaps that may just be the last thing on my list. It is one thing to pursue your goals and another to toil. Toiling is a level where you are beating against the prick.

You are not only catching clouds but are also after vapour that cannot be contained. You fish with a net that is filled with holes, fetching water with a bucket filled with holes. You are catching air with your bare hands. The air is there, but you cannot see it.

I do not want to toil. A fish in water swims. A bird glides. They don't need to be educated to do the very basics. When you toil, you are like a fish trying to sprint on land. It not only costs you a high level of stress but can cost you your entire life.

It would also be nice to have a last bullet on my list. I don't yet know what it is, but I would love to come up with some form of last point on the 'to do' list. I have no idea how I will know that this is the last thing, but I will be relieved to know that this is *it*.

From then on, I may just be emancipated from the list. Perhaps it will come to me unaware, like spotting a shoe you need when you were not even planning on going shopping.

Maybe it will be like reading one more page and another of a page-turner and reaching an abrupt halt halfway in the chapter. You read and suddenly your subconscious jilts. Your soul whispers 'enough' and your being replies 'okay'.

Just like that, you are delivered. Just like that, you are weaned. You are no longer a traveller, for you have reached your destination. There is no journey any more, you can unpack.

Just like that, you no longer have the urge to reach for the bottle or comfort food. There is no war within you. There is no more turmoil in your psyche. This is the envisioned moment that you doubted would ever come true.

The addiction is gone. You are not as you used to be. You are free. You have come full circle.

You come to the realisation that you are going to be just fine. You are no longer a seeker any more but are the very object that you have been searching for. You realise that it was not gold metal but fellow beloveds.

Aha! That's just what I seek right now. I seek it because I have it not in abundance. There is a deficiency of beloveds who are willing to love in spite of disapproving.

I did not know that the colour of the man in my bedroom could affect more than what my body felt. It not only converted me to be his beloved but exposed the racial tensions that existed in his beloveds.

Beloveds love . . . that's what I thought. How deceived was I to think this way! Beloveds love with conditions. A black woman and a white man do not fit those terms and conditions. It is a taboo, an abomination that is jilting more beloved apart, instead of together.

What exactly is this damn *beloveds'* concept that I put together?

Beloved

Trust in the LORD with all your heart and lean not on your own understanding.

(Prov. 3: 5)

Here and there, reality and ideal, current and future—what I feel today may not be what defines me tomorrow. My actions now should never be dictated by the restricting traditions of the past.

The me I am is not the one that longs for a light to be shone. That is the me I will be when the light shines on me, and I am transformed. The me I am acknowledged the greatness within that is longing to be given a chance.

As I write, I fear that the me I will be will not be accepted in this today. Even the current me is not ready for the me that is bursting to come forth out of me. It looks like I am, but I know the present must first die in order to enter into tomorrow.

It is easy to say all sorts of things to fill up the pages, especially when one is nervous. It is even worse to admit that I am nervous. I am petrified of you knowing that I am not in control as I jot this down.

I am not in control because the me that I am and the me I know I can be are at war. There is a war within me that is stretching me and cornering me to let go of the status quo and rewrite my existence.

I don't want you to think that my emotions are weak. Right now, they are my strength; I guess we both just don't know it yet. Still, there is a discontented unrest that stems from opening up about this.

I am not a person that is distinctly drawn by emotion. Expressing emotions freaks me out. There are the usual emotions and then there are those that talk without words. A glance that says it all.

There are emotions beyond emotions, like a sigh that expresses fatigue beyond belief. A hum that takes off when words fade. Take this chapter as a hum. Take it as a melody. The sound of an instrument. A trumpet all cleaned out and shiny.

This chapter is like the banging of the African drum. It is the sound my drum is making right now as it is given a voice and translated into the words of speech. It is in itself an injustice. It is somewhat incomplete and longing to be whole.

Let me scrap off the loaded jargon and start beating the drum. In order to get music, I need to kill animals, skin them, eat their meat, and staple their skin to the drum.

I don't give a damn about what the world says about everything. The opinions out there do not touch me. I have filters in place that determine what is allowed to move from out there to in here.

I care when it comes to a man who I believe was sent to me by God. From the very first conversation, he got me. Not in a literal sense, but in a manner far deeper than any physical touch.

I remember it like it was yesterday. I was intrigued by the African art thing around his neck. He wore a hat and was rather casual. His profile photo stood out. Something within me was drawn to him.

I don't know what made me say hi. Before I knew it, one greeting led to another. One word for another. A phrase. A sentence. A conversation was birthed. Looking back, it is safe to say that that conversation is still going strong. It has gained momentum and is now at full speed.

We met online. It was like, we stumbled upon each other. Before I knew it, we had a very long conversation. We opened up within the very few hours. I spoke to him as a friend.

We interrogated each other. Asked very sharp and grilling questions. His sincerity captivated me and resulted in a lengthy conversation. We are still speaking. I think we are still asking ourselves even more direct questions; the only difference is that this time we are part of the solutions.

I fell in love. It was not the butterfly type of love that buzzes around, longing to be embraced, but one that came with knowledge. I did not fall in love on the first conversation or the second or third; it was over the passing of time.

What connected me to who he was, was not his eyes, his gentle spirit or his possessions that commanded my being to gravitate towards him, it was who he was to me. He was something that I am yet to define. He evoked something in me that I had not yet encountered.

I like to be in control. I need order. It is who I am. He lets me be without compromising on his manhood. He is a man and does not feel intimidated by a successful woman.

He understands that within each powerhouse, at a subtle corner of the lady boss is a delicate girl longing to be loved for who she is. She just longs to be known. That is the desire of her heart. Nothing else. He knows me. I don't know what exactly makes me say this, but I can say this because he knows my strengths and weaknesses that many others are not privy to.

We are in sync to the extent that in loving him, I love myself. He is no longer just an individual out there; he is someone that I care about. There is something in him that my soul celebrates when we are together.

He is not a better part of me or the worst of me. We are so different that one can be justified in saying that he is my better whole. He is the calm, non-temperamental figure that simply gets pleasure from being with me.

When with him, I am not afraid. There is no room for fear. His presence dissipates shadows and reassures me that he is here. His very presence brings a smile to my being.

I strip off the make-up, unplait the hair, and put on my slippers. I do not need to dress up to retain him. I don't even need to say a lot of words that I don't know what they mean. It is not about what is projected, but what is real.

Is he my knight in shining armour? Is this *the one*? Could he be another beloved one? I wish I could write with certain conviction that this is it. I wish I could raise my arm up high as I did in high school when I knew the answer.

I would give anything to forecast the novel ending the way I want it to, but I would be lying to you. Even worse than that, I would be lying to myself. That's the worst lie; to lie to yourself and try to convince yourself of something that you know is not the truth.

I do not want to deceive myself. This is not a novel but a slice of life. Novels are born in the heads of their authors. This one is not a novel. It is about me, my beloved and children.

I guess all I am graciously trying to say is that I don't know if this is *it*. I don't know if this man—of a different race, appearance and upbringing—is all that I fathomed fairy tales to be.

Right now I am not even sure what this fairy tale is supposed to be. I am reassessing the entire notion of fairy tales. I don't know where it comes from or what its purpose outside of entertaining children is supposed to be.

I can tell you that which I know. This is what I know for sure: I do know that he makes me smile. I do know that I feel at ease when I am with him. I know that he slows down my breathing and makes it spin out of control with a peek.

I can tell you without a splinter of a doubt that when I am having one of those days where I find myself pleading with earth to open up and swallow me; even then, he makes me feel a lot better.

When he wraps his arms around me, time is ours to command. Time is subdued. Nations are ours to control. We own the domain. Nothing really matters any more. We kiss in slow motion, and all my senses are receptive to his delicate touch. Right there, time retraces its steps.

The territory is transformed into a dance studio. We dance in sync, even without music. We become the music. Our bodies evolve into notes. We beat the drum into a fusion that reminds us that we are all just human beings.

Is this the love of the mythical heroes? Could this be the love that causes earth to rotate on its axis just a little bit slower so that I can take it all in? Is this the real stuff that cannot be water washed and enacted to end when the episode ends?

I don't know.

I wish I knew. I wish I could skip in and out of time to take a good look and then come back and report to you. Then again, I am glad I do not know because each day keeps me glued to my seat, wondering what will unfold.

Does such love grow cold? Can such love that fills the room with a tangible presence actually freeze? Do I want this so bad that I am imagining it? Is he real? How do I know that he is the real deal?

You see what I mean? There I go again, asking questions that are asked but rarely verbalised. The objective reassures me that I would be crazy for not asking these questions.

I don't want you to think that I care for him. Not care, but care very deeply to the extent that I would be sad if things did not work out between us. I would most likely hide it well and continue to be the responsible career woman that I am.

You would most likely not see the sadness in my eyes, but truth be told, I would be sad. I would hide it well and continue to work as I always do. I would work harder to keep busy and hide the sadness.

I am sad, even as I think, because there are so many obstacles that stand between us from the mere reality that he is of a different complexion. Let us remove the politically correct speech and just be straight forward.

He is white, and I am black.

Here is a man for whom there is questionably very little I would not do for his well-being and who I know would do anything for me. I know this because every day he is with me, and he loses out on others close to him.

I am sad that in being with me, his intimate relationships with loved ones are compromised. It breaks my heart to note that had we both had the same hair texture, he would not constantly have to choose.

In loving him, I love all that is dear to him. I love even those who despise me for loving him because they mean a lot to him and so they matter to me. I love even those that hate me for all that I represent.

They do not hate me for me, but for the heritage my rich, dark skin represents. They hate my people, and I am part of that collective. They despise me because I am a reminder of the power they lost. I am now perceived as wanting to take away their son.

Those that want me banished do so without even knowing my name. It was not about me in terms of my character but the colour of my skin. I am rejected for accepting the call to love a love that transcends physical and racial divide.

Even though I am not allowed in the presence of those who are disgusted by two ordinary people adoring each other against all odds,

I continue to raise a white flag for the sake of peace and for the man I love.

I am depicted as being at fault for being black and loving a white man. Do blacks need permission or rituals to engage with whites on an intimate level? Am I being sidelined for caring? I am just as baffled about my alleged 'crime'!

It is easier to let him go. Yet letting go of him would be like letting go of myself. I love him. I know that he loves me. Love is always worth believing in. It is something untainted that longs to be embraced even against all odds.

If loving him is the biggest mistake of my life, I choose to love him and love him until there is no breath left in me; for it would be a life well spent. It would be a fruitful and meaningful life of knowing that for once, I was loved and I loved.

Sometimes I ask myself: why am I so hated for loving someone? Why does the rejection get personified so clearly? It is not make-believe hatred, but one that is tangibly real.

How can the same God who made all races bar specific people from others? How can brethren and sisters in Christ not imitate his love that gives us second, third, and seventy-seventh chances?

There is strong opposition. I don't mind the strong opposition coming from the world. I am prepared for the strong opposition that comes from out there. I can take on and blow up a nameless opposition. It is the enemy that has a face and is in our own camp that most paralyses me.

I cannot fight because I am not able to self-destruct. Taking on family and friends—loved ones in every sense—who have positioned us as foes because of our mixed relation would be suicidal. It would eliminate the biased tension but hurt very much.

I have asked myself in the middle of the night when he is not there if all this unwarranted enmity is worth it. I don't understand it. I don't want to fight when my intention is to love. Hate is not the solution. It has never prevailed because hate is based on fear.

I know that we are different, but we are willing to be known so that we can eliminate the unknown and the fear that comes from not knowing. Fear comes from losing control. Fear comes from not being secure in your world.

Fear comes from making out an ally to be an enemy. You arm yourself and prepare for a battle, unaware that you are in the same camp. In pulling the trigger or blowing the cannon, you self-destruct.

In hurting that which a loved one loves, you hurt love. You take away from self. You are suicidal. You not only kill your partner but along with his death comes your pain that cannot be silenced.

There is no way you can release a toxic gas into the atmosphere and not expect it to fill your lungs and poison even the unborn generations within us. It is not so much what happens out there that matters, but what we allow into our very own spaces.

I want to be known.

Know my name. Give me a name. Let me be treated according to my conduct. Judge me by my actions, the words from my mouth, and who I am in this moment in time.

I know I may sound a bit cliché, but so be it. It has been said, but let it be said again from the mountaintops. As Martin Luther so gracefully put, 'Judge me by my character and not the colour of my skin.'

When I step out in love, I am not only stepping on to that mountain to project the me that I am becoming. The reality is I am replacing that mountain with self. I am transforming.

I am the mountain.

I am at a higher altitude when I love than when I opt for discarding people who have discarded me because of the colour of my skin. Even when it is causing a war, love presses on.

I am not calling out for mercy. I am resolute in my standing and will not be moved in my stance of deciding to love. So what if he is white? So what if I am black? You need both black and white keys to make unforgettable music on the piano!

Together, we are like a grand symphony that sings on the mountain top. The clouds and higher hosts of heaven stand in awe when they see us and gather up. They shake and rattle in amusement. It rains when we kiss.

Rather than rejecting us for having found one another, teach us to incorporate change. Hold our hands and let us navigate this unmarked territory together. Love does not reject; it accepts and always has room to love one more in the purest of ways.

Let us learn to bring about a revolutionary kind of love together. You can withhold your love; you can withhold your money and possessions, all that can be replaced. Just don't withhold yourself.

Let us be known for loving and being disciples of love. Let us be known for being a woman and man who taught communities that it is okay to love and be loved.

There is no erring in loving. The big err comes in shutting your heart and teaching it to divide. The mistake comes when we tighten our fists instead of opening up our hands to be embraced.

All people are worthy of love. A touch is not one that is restricted to physical touch but a presence. Do not withhold your presence, for there cannot be another like you on this earth.

Dear beloved, let's love one another. Love covers a multitude of sins. Love ushers in grace when doctrine rebukes all that is unknown. Doctrine does not accept any opposing points of views. Love collects ordinary people and sets them apart as extraordinary.

I am not vouching for peace because I am scared of war. No, I am ready for battle. Ready for combat. However, I opt for love because war divides, but love has room for everybody.

In loving him, I reprimand the me that longs to defend myself and gracefully take on a seemingly impossible task of voting for love even when it does not look like the obvious and popular contender.

I am on the side of love. I have made the decision to cross the great divide to dance in the side of love. So much so, I am now a disciple of love. There is conviction that resides in my gut.

I do not care about being right or wrong. I am not on the warpath. I am advocating for unity for the sake of love. I wish to be known. I wish to know that which I love and continue to love with renewed understanding. That's the key ingredient right here: understanding.

Understanding knows and even when it does not, it seeks to do so. I wish to know. I wish to know so that I can educate myself and the people around me. I am not only after understanding to be extended to me, I want to also give it away.

I wish to be corrected in love so that I can teach myself and learn how to be, when in the situation that is outside of my comfort zone. I want to be able to stand in all situations because I am grounded in love alone.

I don't want you to know that it makes me very sad that I can be accepted for who I am when it comes to career objectives, yet, rejected for being with the one my soul dances in delight when he is around.

It devastates me that while the gross majority of the land is over racial stereotypes and prejudices, my very presence, his very presence, is still perceived as a threat.

The fact that two people can dare to go against social constructions in the pursuit of love makes a few feel uncomfortable and angry. It breeds discontentment. Real anger. Hatred.

Some of our beloved have taken it upon themselves to cast us aside. They have made it their mission to make this a lesson to be remembered. Banish us as a sign and warning for anyone else in future to learn that blacks should not mix with whites.

The banishment is a token of fear to teach younger generations that what we are doing is wrong. It is a form of control that draws a line to exclude and make it clear that it will not be tolerated.

Racial tolerance is still seen as a way of pushing against the grain. Love is restricted to certain colour schemes and is not projected as love but the contrary when it dares to love another race in an intimate way.

Rather than strengthening its existence, it is seen as watering down a culture. It is projected as weakening a group and threatening to discontinue perfect seed. The notion of merging two people is one that is not allowed.

The potential of coloured children, sharing your identity with another race and opening up your doors is not welcome. It suggests the horror of giving away your surname to someone with different looks and sharing your legacy: all that calls for fear.

The reality is that I am not as much after a surname but just want to be with the man I love. I don't want him to lose his beloveds just because he is with me. I don't want him to be positioned as an outsider or one without origin simply because he chose to love.

Let us stop advocating for world peace and all those fancy names but genuinely start tolerating each other. The foe is not out there but in our very homes and cities.

Is it not love that loves against all odds? Is love not as powerful as life that it should be embraced by the living? Is love not meant to capture broken people and make them whole again?

Is love not worthy to be called love only when it survives the test of time and stands against strong adversity? Here is strong opposition, and I can tell you that this love is still standing.

Love is one that triumphs. Love conquers all. Love nests itself in humble beings and makes them immortal. Love whispers frailty that softens up even the hardest of souls. Only love can call foes as fellow beloved.

He makes me happy. I would never deliberately hurt him. I think I love him. I think I love him a whole lot more than just 'think'. Allow me to make this correction: I know.

I know I love him with every fibre in my being. We have surpassed the level of I *think* I am in love. I am just deeply hurt that our love is causing such a great chasm with some we love and who love us.

Treat me as horribly as you want. Be ruthless with us. Just don't let our young beloveds ever think that it is okay to hate others without knowing them. Please just let our children be happy and free.

Don't cloud up the minds of children with intolerance. Children are colour-blind. They are born free. You may not know it, but they are impressionable and tend to believe what they are told by those they look up to.

They look up to their beloved. Believe it or not, we also look up to our beloved. It is just that we can take the separation and distinguish that true love protects and does not throw tantrums when it does not get its way.

There needs to be a distinction in the battles of adults and those of children. Let us leave it to the adults. Children need love. A love that is from the heart of a parent to them.

Infants and toddlers along with all children out there need to be grounded on a love that is not restricted to colour. A love that won't alter with looks but comes from the position of love for a child, whether one from your own loins or the love of a beloved.

I was loved by a dad who stepped up and redefined the very concept of what a dad meant. He was not my biological dad. Yet, he was my dad in every sense. In loving me, he loved his beloved, that being my mother.

My mother was loved by his deeds that surpassed her and overlapped into all other facets and areas that were of significance to her. He did not just love her but made an effort to understand her.

In understanding her, he understood that loving her was loving her completely. In loving her family, he loved her. There was more to love than just loving his beloved.

In caring, being there, and being all that a dad should have been, he raised a warrior in me that refuses to be silenced by the injustice of a loveless situation. I was loved by a man who knew I was not his biological daughter and did not give a damn. He chose to love me, regardless.

Love does not force one to choose. Even after my beloved has chosen to be with me, I am not boastful. I do not rub it in the face. It saddens me because the real competition here should be for tolerance and nothing else.

I am not after an earthly inheritance that can be purchased with money but call for the emancipation of paradigms to be shifted. I am not one that stands as a catalyst, ready to dictate change, but one that is in the frontline of danger.

I am here as one most vulnerable and eager to adapt, learn, and change for the sake of protecting the sacredness in the minds of children who should not be allowed to ever think that hate; unwarranted hate is ever okay.

Once again, I ask myself if he is worth it. I ask my conscious mind if he is worth all this tension and division. Why am I allowing this man to continue to capture my heart when being with him brings all this drama?

The answer resides within me. I believe that God sent him to me. I can reassure myself that when he came into my life, I was not even aware that I was lacking. I just know that I am not lonely any more.

I am not in need of anything other than to be in his arms. I do not desire possessions that I do not have or wealth outside of what has already been given to me. It is not about things, but Liefling.

When he holds me, all the questions and answers hush. There is silence. A resetting takes place. It is all worth it. I de-arm. I not only lower my weapons, I cast them down and refuse to pick them up.

All of me collapses. There is a certain faintness that emerges. I no longer give a damn about being right. I just want to be his and him to be mine. I am not longing for this on my own but am merely stating what I believe is our united plea.

I long to try all I can to reunite people. It is not a battle against the world but one over the domination of the mind of ordinary people like me. I long to break the silence and release a sound, even if it is a whisper into the atmosphere.

In his arms, I transform into a lover. I give up my gender, race, and all that sets me apart and simply become his beloved. I take on the identity of the one who loves him more than I ever thought imaginable. I relinquish my titles and executive career stances and transform into a woman held by her man.

When he holds my little girl—I know that he loves me. As he makes my beloved, his beloved, I am answered. There are no questions that can stand against that.

Even the questions I did not ask receive their answers. Mine is not to replace the living. Mine is not to take on roles that are already filled. I can and will love to the best of my ability.

I command the hurt within me to stop. I dictate to the rejection militating against him to be subdued. The warrior in me arises. A helper in me emerges, ready to help her partner. He is my partner.

The goddess in me takes a stand on the mountain top. She runs with bare feet that tread upon the earth. She stands and refuses to waver. She does not quiver or move. I retain my ground.

A knowledge I cannot deny overwhelms me. A truth I know convicts my bruised emotions and commands me to fall on my knees in submission. I choose to fall on my knees.

I fall not to any man, but facedown I fall as the light within me reconnects to Light. In spite of it all, in the midst of it all, through it all, I know that I choose love. I choose love all over again.

A truth I know captivates me. It draws me to retain my place on the mountain top. I see clearer than I have ever seen before. I see further from the mountain top. I refuse to be moved and fall down because of the here and now.

I know something: this I know is true. It contradicts the here and now but remains unquestionably true. My beloved's beloveds have become my beloveds. He has become mine and I am his.

I also know that his brokenness is now mine. The remnants of pain that stemmed from our previous separation are ours. We have both been married. We are both parents even before we met. We have given up before.

Can two divorcees survive the call of this new relationship along with the drama around us over our multiracial aspects? Our track record is not the best. It is one thing to say that we are not our past. Yet, can we hold even when fellow beloveds turn away and call for a recall of our love?

Two Broken Vessels

As iron sharpens iron, so one person sharpens another.

(Prov. 27: 17)

I am a divorcee and so is Liefling.

In as much as society tries to rationalise it; it feels distorted. You move from feeling messed up and just can't help to ask yourself if you are the one that is messed up.

You start thinking that maybe, just maybe there is something unlovable within you. In the end, you wonder if the unlovable part within you is not the reason that you are no longer together. You stop feeling worthy of love and figure that maybe you got what you deserved.

Let's be blatantly honest; marriage is not like returning a pair of faulty shoes. It is not as easy as going back to the shop to return damaged goods. It is not as easy as handing in a receipt and returning with your money or another pair of better fitting shoes.

You return a person. You return yourself. It is like trying to force back a child into the womb; that can never happen. You do not regroup people and call the witnesses to say that we lied to you all when we said that we would love until death.

Even the vows you said did not cater for such a moment. You are both very much alive and separated before death. You never do *un-vow*.

You promise the world in your vows. You promise this and that in the most poetic way.

Divorce makes it clear that you lied or something went terribly wrong. You vowed in public and divorced in secret because it is an embarrassment. It is an experience where you realise that you have not only let yourself down, but many others as well.

Unlike your wedding day when you made the vow and signed very happily, you don't even dress up and make it a special day to divorce. I tell you; it is a painful thing. It is not all it is cracked up to be.

Even when you meet another, there is never a place where you stand before the entire congregation like you did with the first marriage and shout, 'I lied. I am still alive, I am not dead, but my life partner is no longer with me. We lied to you. We lied to ourselves. We lied to our children and the unborn children that were still hoping to come out from our union.'

As the marriage sinks, it sinks with a part of your soul. Something within you alters, chops, and changes when you are the damaged good that is being returned. Even when you are the one calling it quits, it hurts to see someone give up on you.

This is worse than death because it is the death that happens among the living. It is the death that penetrates vows and nullifies all you swore. You give up on the part where you believed yourself. You stop believing in the person that was in your most inner, intimate circle.

You kind of feel like a failure. That is an understatement, you feel like a flop. Even the little ring around your finger was not a token of eternity as you said it would be. You painfully take it off and hide it. You are not wanted any more. You are divorced.

In as much as people say that it is not that bad, it is. In fact, it is worse than what it is said to be. You no longer know what can hold you any more. Vows give in. Contracts have escape clauses. Children are shared.

Nothing seems to be as it appears. You just don't know what you can count on or where you can stand because you realise there is a lot of sinking sand that is disguised as rock solid material.

I think it was the divorce that reignited my faith. When all else proved to be sinking sand, I no longer sang the hymn but truly believed with all my heart that Christ Jesus alone is the rock upon which I stand and all other ground is none but sinking sand. Yes, all other ground, regardless of how it is presented, is sinking sand.

After a divorce, it is not easy to fall in love again. You doubt yourself and don't believe others as you used to. The believer in you is hit with a jab and can decide to stay down or to try and get up again.

You ask yourself, what type of love is this that fails when it was believed that it would not fail? What type of love is this that falls off when the road gets bumpy and drowns in the water?

On the one hand, you open up your soul and body to a very deep connection with your life partner, but there's that little fear that you have to confront on a daily basis.

When you lose your life partner, it is like losing life itself.

You lose the one whereby it was pronounced that the two are no longer two, but one. You lose yourself. You have yourself reject yourself. You give up on yourself. Your innermost shrine and intimacy is defiled. You doubt yourself or whatever is left.

The reason you doubt is because you no longer know who you are. You do, but another living part of you is gone. A part of you no longer tolerates being together. A dream dies. All the hopes of yourself and your other self, the communities, and congregation seem to fall flat.

The vow made in all soberness does not hold. It dares to resemble a lie. Something changed that should have been static. Something gave in; something collapses when it should have stood tall.

Brokenness cannot be disguised.

It is sometimes camouflaged, but it glows even in the dark. It stands out. It is not a pretty sight, especially when it is covered up and disguised. Even when you hide it behind, working ten times as hard at work, the void it leaves behind continues to chase you and cause scary shadows to torment you.

I am aware of the fact that there is more counting on daring to love again when you have already been bruised. You come in with insight and unwarranted fears, and it is an act of bravery to love again.

You are cognisant of the fact that true unconditional love is indeed the greatest. You are more serious because a lot is counting on this. You are supposed to be wiser and braver. Love is indeed an act of courage. It is a gift from God. Another chance and a Holy dominion.

Rather than approaching this as the masters of love, Liefling and I are two broken vessels that come together to form a beautiful artwork. We are art. Craftsmen that carve out using our guts.

We are two creators that create something out of recycled shreds of heart. We recycle hope. Patch it up and stitch it together to form something glorious out of discarded material. Discarded people.

It sounds harsh, but in some way it is so. People gave up on us. We gave up on people. There were instances where it seemed that there was no hope at all. Restoration gave up in us. We gave up on ourselves. This is not so any longer. Love gave us a second chance.

In some way, you sometimes wonder if the giving-up took place too soon. You ask yourself if it is justified to ever write someone off. Rule out the living as though paths never merged.

There was a point of intersection. Rather than get together and merge, the paths crossed. They still continue on another separate axis. They come together here and there for matters concerning the children, but that is just about it.

When someone that you entrust yourself to on such a deep level is no longer there, something within you leaves your psyche. The bed grows exponentially bigger. The silence is magnified. It personifies. It walks with you. It enters the bedroom with you. It showers with you.

Silence forms a being that dwells within you. This being has a name but won't tell you because it is formed out of silence. This silence wants to talk to you, but silence is not allowed to talk. It merely stands there and gazes at you.

You don't want it because you know it comes from loss, but there is no way you can rule it out. You see the silence, and it sees you. You touch the silence and realise you have just touched yourself. Then something clicks. You know that this is true: you are that silence.

Silence is often seen in nature, but not to this proportion. One moment there is sun, the next it is gone. The sun rays were fleeting. They were there, hot and healing and the next moment, you are in the dark.

You can barely locate yourself. You are crippled in your vision. Even what is right in front of you gets concealed by the darkness. Darkness magnifies its presence. If there is no light, darkest darkness will persist.

It is not that things are not there any more, they are there. You can just no longer see them. When the silence consumes you, even you seem invisible to yourself. You look invisible in the cover of a pitch night.

Others can't see you. You can barely see yourself. Yet, even though you look like you are not there, you know you are. Your heart faintly pants for someone to take notice of you.

It is easy to hide in the night. It is easy to think that this is it. Yet, a pulse cannot be concealed. Life cannot be denied a chance to express itself and live. Whether you are seen or in hiding, you cannot be hidden.

The sun relocates from your world and chooses another. It knows you need it and cannot continue to live in the dark without it, but it goes.

Just when you think it is established and cannot fall, it departs from you. The sun votes against you.

The sun relocates and does not take you with it. You plead with the sun to stop but then realise it is part of the sun's destiny. You are not able to follow. This is where your journey stops.

You chase it but cannot keep pace. You cry after it and entice it with poetic words and eventually offer all of yourself to see just one more ray. The ray never returns. It is gone, just like your marriage.

The temperature drops. The night falls in the absence of day. One moment you were in day, and the next, you arrived at night. It is where you are. Sun is gone. Warmth has suddenly disappeared. Vision is blurred. There you are.

There you are all alone. You are back to where you started. Alone again. This time, it feels a lot harsher because unlike the sun that left and will return in the morning; this will most likely not be the case for you.

Nothing will happen in the morning. Even the sun relents. The sun reconsiders and comes back. It cannot stand to see you alone without it. It knows you need it and so it returns.

Unlike the mood-swings of the sun that causes day-and-night alterations, divorce is not like that. In most cases, it is final. It takes no casualties but consumes all you were. You cannot come out the same. No one does. It transforms your essence.

You are not as you were. Yes, you have been alone before. You have been here before, but you may not return to that stance. Before the marriage, you were single. You were full of potential. Even that identity of being 'single' is loaded. Now, you are no longer that, you are divorced. You often realise that you are the remnant of whole.

War seems great from afar. You fight for little badges to stick on your uniform. The reality is that bullets hurt. Smoke chokes up human lungs.

The wear and tear takes its toll on the body. Emotions erupt until they are forced down and harnessed.

It is almost like running to a city of refuge because you are wounded and can no longer be in battle.

No one marries to divorce. If you do, there's something controversial about you. I do not know a single person who would go all out to inconvenience themselves in this manner for the sake of doing it for fun.

No one dreams of being a divorcee. Even fairy tales dictate that you are supposed to live happily ever after. Ever after is not supposed to carve in when the winds rage. Knees are not supposed to bend when the storm batters against you.

Houses are designed to stand. Foundations are meant to hold. Love is supposed to endure. Divorce is the fall. Divorce is the weakening that could not be reinforced in time. It is the thing you hear least preached about.

Love songs sell. Novels on love sell. You find bestsellers on love and the epics of true love. Few want to hear about how something collapsed and consumed a union as powerful as death itself.

Broken vows are not spoken about. If they could be described, they would be sung as an elegy. They would be interpreted in tears and utter brokenness. It would be like shattering a diamond into many particles longing to come together, but not knowing how.

Divorce sucks.

Yes, it is empowering, freeing, and all that you want to say it is, but it is scary. A part of you hopes it does not happen again. A part of you fears that you have this fear in the first place because you know you will gravitate towards all that make this fear a reality.

You fear that if it has happened before, maybe it will happen again. It is said that lightning does not strike at the same place twice. Is divorce equivalent to lightning?

After my lengthy separation, I sought to find myself. Ask myself the tough questions only I could answer. Role played with me for none other than me and tried to learn from my mistakes and those of others.

Rather than just rushing to hide the void, I took my time to find myself. Reinforced the knees. I took time to get to know myself and love myself anew. I did not want to fall apart or keep it together. I just wanted to heal.

My goal was to break down my emotional house and start from scratch. Build a much deeper foundation. Assess the damage. Recycle what I could. Salvage the good and discard the weak elements.

The thought was survival. The quest was not to run but to learn to breathe again on my own. On an external level, work and other relations could not have been better.

Divorce is none other than death. Your heart beats as though it forgets that you are dead. That is most probably the only sane thing about it. Your heart continues to beat.

It is not even the explanations, trying to explain that we lied at the altar, or shock from others. There's nothing more to say other than I died. Just like that, I was no more.

Fortunately with death comes resurrection. The old me died, but something totally new arose from the seed. A seed was planted and it died. I arose with renewed and multiplied strength. It was not an instant shoot but a very tough process.

Personally, I was hanging on a thread. It took a lot to reinforce my heart to get it to a level of beating and functioning again as humans are supposed to. It was simply about fortifying my gates. Rededicating my temple. Purging my core.

I never thought that my heart would be tender again. There was a time when I did not think it would even be possible. While I am glad that love remembered my name and gave me someone incredible to be with, I find myself at the crossroads once again, urged to choose.

I want to choose the safe route. I want to choose someone and something that will embrace me and never give up on me. I want to choose the easy path because I am downright tired of 'character building' stunts that keep breaking me down.

I know that going for Liefling is not necessarily the easy route that I envisioned. There are many underlying struggles that stem from me being black and the hard-headedness of people.

I cannot change who I am. Should I just go for someone else who looks a whole lot like me? I do not want to lose myself again. I want to be found and never ever lost. I really don't know if I should stay with the man I love or settle with a man who loves me—whom, in turn, I will respect and love for being a devoted husband.

Unwanted, Again

My son, if sinful men entice you, do not give in to them.

(Prov. 1: 10-11)

It is easy to call the sky blue. You ignore the grey particles of dust hushing past and discard the presence of foamy whitish, silvery clouds. You disregard the presence of birds floating about in the cold sky and the discolouration that they add thereto.

They are not just adding to the colour spectrum, they are the sky. It seems incomplete without all these living and static objects living in the sky. It seems undone. There's something more that needs to be traced in and coloured in.

It is like an incomplete painting or sculpture that never was because it never began. It calls out to the madness of writing theories and setting up galleries to celebrate and exhibit the sculpture that has not yet been created.

It calls out to her majesty, trying to evoke that which has never been alive. Conjuring the spirit of one without a host to arise and emerge to the sky. Soar anew when it has never been. It is a crazy celebration of what is not. A figment of imagination puffed up to enormous proportions. It harkens to madness.

In spite of all that the sky is and is not, it is still easier to call it blue. Why do we not say, the sky is a great chasm? The sky is a void filled with particles of dust that look blue. The sky, like the bark of a tree, is not the totality, but part of something bigger.

The sky is not that which we think it is. It is not, because it is what it is. Only the sky can attest to being a gas or substance or maybe a host. The sky alone knows exactly what it is.

At times, the sky may not know, but the creator of sky, who has the blueprint, knows best. The sky and the inhabitants of the earth may question it based on human intelligence and totally miss the divine plan.

From a superficial level, it is there to host birds that take off to levels man only dreams of. It is host to drifters without feet. It does not have solid land to plant roots. It is lost, more lost than it has ever been before.

The sky is blue. Call it by what you see. It is easier to call things by what you see. It is easier to look at the surface and segment according to stereotypes. Let us discard all else that you see in the sky or hold the sky to be and simply say that it is blue.

Here's another confession that comes out as slippery as saying the sky is blue: I am black and Liefling is white. No one has ever seen a black person. No one has ever seen a white person. It is these very social constructions that add to a distorted identity.

Show me a living black person other than one who is beaten up black and blue or is dead and tarnished beyond recognition.

We all have red blood. Life is in the blood. That blood can be transfused from one person to another. Hearts are the same. They can move from one dead being to awaken another. Vital organs, those that give us life can be shifted from one being to another. There is more that unites us than the aesthetics that separate us.

Black is generally understood to be the colour of mourning. In many societies, black is the colour of death. People who are weeping and mourning wear black. When one is having a funeral, a black flag can be seen pitched against the blue sky. Black calls out to evil and the night.

Children have an innate fear of darkness and the pitch-black night. Brides do not generally opt for black, but white. If black signals weeping, white whispers celebration. A white flag dances and shouts that there is a joyous celebration.

Heaven is engulfed with the notions of light and pure white, spotless garments. White is the colour of virginity, cleanness, and superiority. Where black is associated with the night, white is regarded as purity and light.

Unless we address the notion of identity and what it means to be black or white, we are in no position to continue the way that we have. We are merely planting seeds of destruction that are bound to blast out the neat exterior and expose the junk within.

Junk calls out to junk. It is such identity misrepresentations that need to be redefined. I am African and am proud of it. We are as we ought to be.

As a young couple, along with the nation as a whole, we need to personally sit down and redefine what that means to us. We can no longer tolerate the historic representations of that in this modern society.

White can in no way continue to be regarded as master and black as slave. In as much as this does not seem to be the case in urban cities, it needs to filter down to the little towns and unknown settlements nestled in the inner and secluded folds of our majestic South Africa.

We are not one.

Unless we can all have the same translations derived from the same connotations, there can never be unity. Unless we speak in all our languages and derive at the same meaning, we cannot stop talking. Perhaps we should change the way we talk, but the talking itself is needed more than ever.

One cannot see black diamond as an absolute treasure while others see black as a curse. Unless we walk together, we will fall prostrate unwillingly.

Let's stop talking about people out there and statistics gathered from anonymous names. Allow me to give you a slice out of real life. Whether it falls within or outside the domains covered by the statistics is irrelevant.

Take me and Liefling; ignore all that you think you know about faceless people. Here are two people with an identity. Two people with faces and emotions.

Regardless of what we have achieved thus far, and being committed citizens in our own ways, we are judged by the colour of our skin. This is not an isolated incident. This is not something that happens to us because we are special. The contrary is true.

It is what is continuing to happen and will reoccur unless we command the spotlight to shine again and dispel this great darkness. Unless we ignite a beacon and call for light, this will continue and the majority of responsible citizens will not even know that it ever took place.

As parents, we individually and mutually take care of our children inherited from past relationships. We love them as best as we can. We are there for them. Sometimes we miss the mark and don't get it right, but we try and are committed to giving parenthood our all.

In as much as there is no perfect parent and we don't profess to be such, we can attest to being there and here—trying, continuously learning, and willing to love our children.

Love means respecting others. It often means accepting the sky and its complexities for what it is. Celebrating its blueness, the birds and life within it. Accepting its grey, white and black aspects, and acknowledging that we need all that to have the sky.

Love means seeing the majesty of the night sky crowned in sparkling lights from the sky. Love means acknowledging the night and the day. Realising that we cannot have day if there is no night. That night is not inferior to day. The same sky facilitates day and night. It is united.

Love means looking beyond skin pigmentations. It transcends caring for the child of your womb to loving another. Being a parent is not restricted to the child of your loins.

Parents love children, regardless of whose children they are. Parents and children need each other, regardless of where we may find ourselves in life.

Here we are. In spite of all the wonder-works written about the progress made, the reality is that our pigmentations are splitting us apart. Where it matters most and by those in our inner circle, we are not judged by our conduct but by the colour of our skin.

My anchor in God has drawn me to find acceptance and strength from a higher dimension. My strength is not in me but in God, who resides within me. I find strength in knowing my true identity in him and knowing that I am loved simply because I am loved. I do not need to enact perfection or to be in perfection, because I am what I am.

When it comes to the spiritual aspects, I am whole. Wholeness is not the absence of fragmentations all around you, but it is finding your centre. Knowing you are ordained to be here by God and for his divine purpose.

It pertains to being whole to the extent that I know who I believe in and do not need to reject others who are of a different belief system or race.

When you know who you are, you are not intimidated by foreign aspects. A different person does not equate into a terrorist prowling in your personal space. You do not fire at the person before triggering a warning shot. Difference is not reason enough to anger one who knows who they are.

I respect difference. I respect diversity because I know that it is needed. It is because we are different that the world we live in instructs us to respect diversity because we are all interdependent on each other.

I know who I am.

I am more than the locks of my hair and my career. In as much as my daughter is my entire life, there is more to me than being a mother. I am more than this moment and my very name. I am not more but all I need to be for this moment.

In spite of all that I am, I am said not to be wanted. To be quite honest, I don't need senseless people in my life. I can do without small minds consumed by racism. I just want it to be known that it is wrong and inhuman to hate other human beings merely because of their skin colour. It reveals despicable characters that have no place in our society. Liefling is unwanted because of his decision to love me—despicable!

Here I am with my heart tender again, and this time, I am unwanted again. I am wanted by the man I deeply care for but unwanted by those whom he deeply cares for.

I have said it before and will say it again: it breaks my heart that in being together, he is set apart and unwanted by those who should rightfully love him based on their blood connections.

It is not everyone who has a problem. Walls don't crumble because of everyone. Cities and revolutions are not started by everyone. It is those few individuals, the exception. It is the little leaven in the dough that causes the entire content within the bowl to rise to great exaggerated proportions.

I see him choosing to be with me. It excites me for a second and then breaks me. It crushes the sighs within me. It is so wrong. He is constantly forced to have a bigger love and a lesser love when love in itself should be adequate.

It hurts me to know that in loving me, he is despised. It is demeaning to recognise that he is rejected, we are rejected, simply because we look a little different to each other. Our features are not the same, but then again, no two people in this world are completely identical.

Again, I find myself unwanted. This time, the colour of my skin is speaking on my behalf. It is speaking to the extent that my name is not needed. I am now 'Die Swart Meisie' the black one. I am unapologetic for being African. It is my pride. A heritage of greatness passed on in the legacy of my genes.

In as much as you cannot expect a child to grow taller or the stars to shine in the presence of the great light of the sun, it is what it is. I am who I am, and there is nothing apologetic in me about that therefore those who can't accept this will have to find ways to deal with it.

I am not the slaves my ancestors were. He is not the master our ancestors feared. He is who he is to me. His presence dwells in my sanctuary. We are lovers. We are not enemies. We are not in eternal combat based on our skins.

I do not love him because of his colour. I love him with his colour. I love everything about him. He is all that to me. I am his, and he is mine. Even if he were the shade of the sun or that of the raging river or earth of majestic mountains, all that he is to me would be none other than the man I love.

For how long can one love the heart when the body and people around you remind you that you are not the same? For how long can knees bend without buckling in?

No one has seen the heart that mankind claims to love with. I am not talking about the physical heart but the heart of our understanding. Is that portion also white? Is it black?

I know it should not matter, but let's face it; almost everything else has been affected by colour. Imagine being with a woman you cannot tell your beloveds about because they will hate you and possibly turn you away . . .

Do I really love him by holding on to him? Should I really hold on to him?

Two Shades of the Same Heart

Where there is no revelation, people cast off restraint; but blessed are those who heed wisdom's instruction.

(Prov. 29: 18)

Life knocks. Hatred answers. Hatred disguises itself with indifference and shuts the door. Hatred calls out to its buddies and peeps through the keyhole to mock life. Hatred sees eyes of life and does not recognise them.

Life knocks on the closed door. Indifference laughs and shuts down unaware that life is the only one who can rescue it from its suicidal tendencies. Hatred makes excuses as to why the door should be closed and fails to perceive that life is none other than love.

Love remains barred. However, there is something about love that transforms. It refuses to be silenced. It cannot be shut down. It cannot be contained. It is like the very air in our lungs. It can make us come alive within ourselves.

When we think we are outside and are external, air meets us there and calls us friends. Even when we are far away from home, air locates us and commands our bodies to live. Grace calls us anew.

Love can never be transformed. Love is immeasurably greater than hate. Love is so much more divine. Even when faced against tough opposition, love protests against death.

Love protests against hate. Love is greater than our cultures that divide us, greater than the walls we hide behind, and greater than the personal constructions we build to protect ourselves.

In loving, we stand together. In loving, we lose our very identity. In loving, we are expelled from that which we thought was love unending. Can love stand when faced with brutal disgust? Can new love birth ancient hope when all else demands for it to let go?

Am I capable of loving a man who shares the same blood as a few who do not want me because of the colour of my skin? It is one thing to imagine and another to know that you are not wanted because your love is seen as a defiance of colour.

Can a tree be uprooted from its origin and planted in foreign terrain? Will that tree flourish without the leaves it knows and the climate that it is accustomed to? I love *Liefling*, and I know that he loves me. It is not something that I think, but I see it in his actions.

He does not need to tell me that he loves me; I know it. I see love. I see it in his actions. It sometimes gets easier to leave, but he comes back. When I come home and see him, as he opens the door, and when I hear his footsteps, love is reinforced. I am overcome with joy as though we just met.

Love simply means holding on even when you have no idea where to go. Love means asking no questions and receiving no answers, but just being there.

I fear for him. I fear for his safety and well-being. Sometimes I ask myself if he does not see if I am black. Can he not see that I am different? Perhaps he does see but is too involved to care less.

He knows that there are slight differences. We have different traditional delicacies. Yet again, people from the same tribe can still like different food. Our taste buds and texture preferences differ.

I know that he is different. He knows that I am not the same. Sometimes, when one sings, the other will laugh. A rural girl and farm boy, all grown up, have very little in common, but everything that matters. Love.

In loving him, I am loved. Love cannot depart and come back void. Love purges. Wet feet on clean carpets mean nothing compared to having no feet to share the carpets with. It is almost as awful as having a feast with no one to join in and add to the great company.

Food without appetite is meaningless. Money without health is futile. All the money and technology in the world cannot restore the will to live. When one has kicked the bucket, all the gold is meaningless. A life without love is not life at all.

He chose me and I don't think I was his first choice. If given the chance, I think he would have chosen to have both his beloveds and me. A couple surrounded by our beloveds.

I could let him go and continue the life of mutual respect that I know, or I could hang on to him and live a life of isolation, watching him lose those closest to him and know that in holding on to me, others will most likely let go of him.

I refused to let him go then, and I will not let him go now. He is to me all that I knew was out there. He is to me what rain is to earth. What sand is to the ocean. What sun is to blue sky. He is nothing but my blue sky.

He does not say much. In saying little, I hear him. I hear him without words. He kisses me without lips. Embraces me without a touch from even the tip of his finger. We speak a language that, in all essence, is not a language at all.

He holds my consciousness and makes it submit to who he is and who I am now that he is here. When he thinks of my little girl, I know he thinks of me. In considering her, he considers me. I do the same for his children, whom I love as my own in my heart.

Is one a loved one because you are of the same blood or are you a loved one because you love? I don't understand how love from those who share his DNA can deny him the beauty of being with the one his soul recognises as someone special.

The reality is that we are not allowed to be together. In being together, we are individually stripped. If you want to see a bloodbath, there is no need to defend the 'Promised Land' or pursue enchantments; simply take me to his home. You will see the 'Armageddon' and rapture all clustered in one.

I am not saying this out of disrespect but as a means of calling out for love to resuscitate the living. Is life and love not precious that we should discard it?

I am not less simply because I am black. I am a human being. I am simply a woman in love with a man. There is nothing more to say.

We are just a normal couple trying to be together and as normal as can be in spite of this ridiculous madness. We have the normal tendencies of any other couple. Sometimes we fight, other times we cuddle. There are no hidden disclosures.

In spite of the country having made enormous steps ahead and no one even thinking that this is still a topic to discuss, here we are. Unwanted without even being known. At the verge of expulsion. I feel like a plant about to be uprooted and cast aside for not complying.

Let me love him. Don't strip him bare for being with a tree of another kind. We are all plantations of some sort.

We need each other. Deal with him for who he is. Don't cast him out because of me. If I am guilty, let it be for loving him with the very breath in my lungs. Let not the love we share break apart the heritage of upbringing, support, and family.

Each day we celebrate our love, we do so in the lurking presence of loss. As we love one more day, as we share one more kiss; tempers arise.

Fury rages. Rage! The cause is how a man can love another across racial and cultural divides. It is absolute madness. Foolishness!

If I could, I would choose to love him anew. If I had no choice, he would still be my innate choice. He is good to me. We are very different, but under the cover of the night, we are just two people, a couple fighting to be together: two shades of the same heart.

Something stirs up inside a man when what he loves is disregarded. It changes who he is. His heart connects on another level in spite of his roots being chopped. It is like nesting on a tree that is being chopped. The petitions were signed and protests held. Yet in spite of it all, the tree is being felled down.

As you nest in the tree, you hear the axe beat against the tree. The cold metal of the iron cuts through the tree's flesh. Various liquids ooze out. There is danger and pain.

It is an illegal eviction, but it is going on. You want to do all you can to protect him. If I could, I would ask, 'Why do you hate me so much? On what grounds do you decide it is right or wrong?'

What wrong have we done? Is love not more precious that it should be esteemed? Do couples not have their own challenges that we should be warring against an army that we cannot inflict or retaliate against because they are composed of people who are located close to our hearts?

Why am I such an abomination to you? The ground whereon you stand is considered holy and the colour of my flesh defiles that. Why are you so afraid to allow love to hold you together when it feels like you are losing all control?

Here's the truth, I am a controlling individual. I see it in the way I want things to be done. I've never been to military but I often want things to be done the military precision. It is in precision that I find comfort. In thoroughness that I am most indulged.

However, this racial animosity has just come to a level I cannot fathom. It is like things have come too far. Words were exchanged that should never have been conceptualised in the first place.

When one is led by racial tension, ideas will arise that should not be there in the first place. Things form that should not be given breath. Conversations live that should have never been conceived.

Yet, even in all this madness, I love him. I know that he loves me by simply being here. Even when it is dictated that we should part. Even when it seems that in being together, we are fighting against customs. It is not so.

We are just two people who found each other and chose to love. We are two colour-blind friends that want to be together even when everything is convincing us to part ways. Even in the midst of temptation, we are standing tall and fighting to be.

We are not fighting people. We are not armed with anything other than the quest to love. The battleground is not out there but in our home, in our intimate space, in the blows we receive, instead of kisses.

We are on the team of love, not breaking up families. We are on the team of building up, not fighting to be. Love does not want to castrate, but love incorporates. Love says the only criterion is a heart willing to be transformed. Here we are, devoted servants of love.

Yet, when one cuts to the root of the matter, you don't find a discussion, but a real war. You find beloved transformed into villains and arch enemies because they just cannot get over the black and white thing.

Our children are being used as tools to infiltrate a love that is still standing. Our greatest treasures—that being our children—are being used to send a strong protest petition to us.

The messages reaching our children cannot stop with the little ones because if you strike down my child with words, you strike me in a magnified proportion. I don't mind being attacked; it is when my child is in danger that the fangs in me come out.

Just when we mastered the strategy of *ignoring the madness that goes on around us*, children were lured in by bitter beloveds. Their vulnerable minds were bombarded with absolute rubbish. Nothing but unfounded words spoken by racists were whispered and shouted into the children's ears. I would expect such deeds from people who have come to realize that they have no future and are in a mission to destroy the next generation's future.

Take all that I have said about waiting for the situation to sort itself out and toss it aside. If you push the 'children button', you have poked the eject seat. Except, I am not leaving this relationship because of racists who wish to control others.

Seeds of Hate

How useless to spread a net where every bird can see it!

(Prov. 1: 17)

Only broods of vipers will bite their own. Rather than teaching the child to fend for themselves and fight, the viper will strike. It will penetrate the veins of the infant. In spite of the scales, death penetrates. It is not something that is taught but an innate characteristic for vipers to strike at each other.

Rather than protecting the weak, vipers slither on. At times the vipers go on in search of their own kind to eat them up. Snakes disregard the weak and fragile eggs.

It is not the big reptiles that matter but that which they impart to the others who look like them and are impressionable. They may look like them, but they are not. They are children, seeds with so much potential in them.

The real tragedy is not that they will look like them. The tragic loss is having these seeds lose who they can become. It is giving up on themselves to take on a cast of racial segregation because of what was instilled within them.

Eggs are casts. They have no shape of their own except that which we give them. They look alike but are not. They contain something pure.

They are unadulterated and pure. It is the big who influence the little ones to hate.

Children are born free. They cling on to anyone who will hold them and love them. They accept and need protection. Not just protection from the defiler but protection from the mind of an enemy with a common face. Protection from physical and non-physical elements.

Children are who they are. In as much as we give off something in ourselves to make them, they come out completely new. They are not just extensions of us but are a whole new breed.

They are not that which we dictate them to be. No matter what we drill down within them, they have the ability to rise above our prejudices if we rewrite that which the canvasses of their minds have soaked in.

A child is born with an innate cry to be loved. There are instances where a lion cub is raised by a buck or even that of a predator raising that which it should be consuming and tearing apart.

The young one does not know that it is different unless it is initiated into a predetermined mould of how to behave and act. If left alone, the babies will play in the playground and sleep together in a cot.

They will gladly eat the food presented to them when they are hungry without being bothered who gave it to them. Adults are the ones who instil fear in these precious souls.

It does not matter who is there, they just want to be comforted and reassured that they are where they should be and things are in order. They need to be reminded that things are in the process of being transformed to work out for their good.

Perhaps it is safe to say that children are born colour-blind. We are the ones who teach them colours. We correct their pronunciations and instil socially constructed understandings and norms.

It is not other children but adults around them that teach them to fear. A child can run on to oncoming traffic without seeing a flicker of danger. We instil fear into their psyche. We command fear to dwell within them as a blanket excuse for protecting them.

Fear.

Fear anything and everyone that looks different. In spite of nature teaching us that diversity is good, we fear change. We fear difference. Rather than embracing the joys of winter, resentment broods.

We postpone our lives and wait for summer. Hope to fast-forward to that which we are accustomed to without realising that there is something I need in winter that spring cannot usher me to.

My body needs night.

There is something magnificent about the many less brighter lights that cause my heart to beat a little slower. There is something in night that calls for a hush, a deeper breath and relief that I cannot find in the haste of day.

We need the covering of darkness to command our bodies to sleep and rest. The air cools off a bit. Light fades. Vision blurs. Rest! Nature orders me to calm down. I am called to shut down and catch my breath.

Unlike in the race of day, I am commanded to see less and therein be less distracted. Night commands my psyche to be at ease. I am tranquilised and reminded to take things a little slowly.

As I sleep, my subconscious awakes. I move from the domain of the conscious mind with man-made limitations to the realm of the limitless subconscious.

As I sleep, the real me awakes. It dances and soars. It surpasses the tensions and man-made stresses to sing with the heavenly hosts in our midst. While sleep captivates my flesh, my soul feels and thinks out solutions.

It is in the night that my mind is most alert. I go further and see solutions. I see a way out. I overcome my handicaps first with my eyes closed and then wake up believing I can.

While sleeping, I hear chants that no words can decipher. They cannot decipher them because these chants are not made for human ears. They are understood by the inner man who has surpassed the wisdom and knowledge of the flesh.

A song bursts within me. It refuses to be kept in the atmosphere and can be heard in here; wherever *here* is. This song is one that is unlike the other songs I have heard people sing. It does not have a voice or a tune. It is a song in its essence.

I sing it in the night. It revives my soul. It nourishes my body. Something inside that is very strong awakes in my weakest and most vulnerable state. Even with eyes shut, I see.

Most of the times, I cannot tell you what I saw when I awake. I just know that I saw. I spoke in a language my very mind does not know. As I spoke, I know that I was not speaking but worshipping.

The *me* I am stood up and took its rightful place. The inner spirit that dwells in my body with a soul took over the body and reconnected back to power. Even while sleeping, something in me quivered; there was locomotion, an earthquake that broke apart the rocks that were blocking my way.

The me I was made to be, stood up and took its rightful place. It shone and just when I thought that it shone, it outshone. It glittered and bedazzled. Even in the night, there was light radiating from within.

I transformed and became the light. The light within me connected to the light in my substance. Together they shone amidst all trials and tensions.

The me that I am conjured with light and became one. There was a union that took place as substances fused and reflected an assortment of lights that thrilled and captivated the living.

The light within me danced and ordered me to dance. My conscious self came out from my subconscious state of being. It connected me to the reality of who I am. By this, I mean the real me, not the me that comes out when in the company of broods, seeking to bite the young.

It is in that state when the real me comes out. It jumps out when it is pinned down. It is when I cannot see with my physical eyes that the eyes of my enlightenment see furthest. They see behind closed doors.

As I write, I close my eyes. I take on the form of a scribe who is inspired by none other than the breath within them. I transform from being who I was to the one I know I was born to be.

Believe it or not, this chapter was not written with the pen or pencil. There were no touch screens or keypads that participated in bringing it to life. It was written in the mind. It was birthed in the spirit. What you see here is a remnant of what appeared when I allowed myself to see without eyes.

Rather than using hands, I lifted my hands before dropping them in a prostrate posture. I gave up my hands in order that I could work at a deeper level that was not confined to my flesh.

The soul in me spoke when my lips stopped moving.

The call in me was answered when I stopped asking my mind. Rather than take on man-made formulas on how to combat this situation, I surrendered. I did nothing and in amputating self, the real inner me was given the grace to express herself.

Her majesty arose in the silence. She arose from my frustrated mind and point of giving up and called for a turnaround. She looked at my-storm battered eyes and said: 'return'!

I recall hearing 'Let there be order'. It was spoken by a presence I know was there but cannot identify. Maybe I am the one that said it. Could it be that I was the one that looked at the situation and commanded order to return and have its dominion.

The boundaries that we set out to restrict others are the very ones that kill us. The snare that I set to catch my brother of another race and creed consumes me.

It snares my mind. It captures my thoughts. It bottles me down until I can only build more snares that chain me down. I do not want the life from our loins to suffer this way. I do not want our beloveds to fall into the trap of fearing those that look different to us.

Seeds—like children—have the potential to multiply. That which is planted grows. Hatred gives birth to death. Segregation leads to death of diversity and death of the mind. Racial discontentment leads to none other than death of self.

The same blood within another is the very one that I need to resuscitate my body. The same hand of another who has a different pigmentation is the one that is able to help me get up when I stumble.

We all stumble from time to time. Even the sun gives way to the moon and stars. It is all part of a good divine plan to allow us to shine as we rightfully should. Today I chose to shine.

Regardless of how the hand looks, soft or otherwise, I hope that will be the hand to help our children when they are lost and cannot find their ways back home. I can only pray for a hand to help me cross the road safely when old and uncertain of my footsteps.

When our children are lost, my desire is that a human hand will reach out to them and stay with them until we are reconnected. I am not so much concerned about the race of the person who will help them because I know that it will be a fellow human being.

I know that that person cares for the children and acknowledges them as weaker ones in need of adult guidance. I know that the hand of the kind stranger is one that has blood and bones beneath the colour of their skin.

It is when our bodies fail us and we are not sure if that which is within us will stand, that we need organs from colourless strangers. Regardless of our differences, we can help to sustain and restore life in others.

It breaks my heart to get looks of disdain from children who are not in approval of a multiracial relationship. I can understand the older generation not being comfortable, but what gets to me most is when young and impressionable children are taught to hate.

Children should be allowed to believe in the good within everyone. They should be given the leniency to believe, without compromising their safety. They should be allowed to believe in fairy tales and happy endings.

No child is born with such disdain. In a transforming world, it saddens me to see leaps in a backward direction. Rather than moving forward, humanity reverses into an era of darkness and fear.

What adults fail to see is that there is something in me and everyone else who looks different and that you need to find your own identity. It is not one specific thing, but a host of yet unidentified necessities that spring out in time of need.

In the same way that there is something in day that I need and something in night that I need, there is that little something peculiar in all of mankind that lies in the other.

It is in the other that I find myself. Without another, I am left wanting. I search but cannot see who I am not. I fear for who I am. When afraid, I dance. As I dance, I transform into something glorious. I am not afraid any more.

Perhaps we need to sing some more. Maybe we need to dance together as different races. We need to connect to the tune of the living and the rhythm of the heart that connects us.

For too long we have been static in fear. We cannot afford to plant hatred in children. Hatred causes them to lose themselves in the shivers caused by fear. Fear binds and constricts. Love releases and dances to the tune of others when it comes into sync with mine.

Let us leave legacies of love. Don't fear me because I am different. In the night, we are all the same. Each embrace from a mother is one that comforts. It is not my looks that matter but the purity of my embrace.

The love of a black mother and a white mother may be expressed differently, but ultimately, they are both from the source of love. When my child is with another who loves them, I can let go and feel at ease.

We need more consciousness to fall flat in order for a higher level of subconsciousness to arise and propel us to greater heights. I need day and I need night to locate me into the time of day.

I need people who know what it is like to be discarded, to stop accepting that and say, I am somebody. I need transitions of greatness that are willing to look at dead situations and command life to return.

Only people can resuscitate people. Only love can stop cycles of hatred. My brother with another skin is still my sibling. My Liefling with different textured hair is my heartbeat.

Sometimes, he lends me his heart and replaces it with mine. Other times, we forget which heart belongs to whom and just celebrate the music it brings with it. His music and mine differ, but they are both much appreciated and unique forms of expressions.

All I want is for our children to get through this. Please don't poison them. I want them to see that I am black and that he is white, but that it does not matter because there is love in the home. Through the passing of time, I know they will recognize no colour but Mom and Dad.

Please don't inject them with venom. They are young and impressionable.

I do not only love my biological daughter as my own. I can't switch between being mom now and then stop if the child is not of my own. Love knows no boundaries. Leave the children alone. I need them in my life.

Here I am, take *me* on anytime.

Try to crush my will to live.

Soften the blows or strengthen them to kill and cause harm. Ridicule, belittle, or distort as you please. Do that which you wish and even more. Bend and remove. Banish and praise.

One thing that I can reassure you is that nothing will take away my innate desire to love. It is as fundamental as the need to have air within your being. What you may or may not know is that children need mothers and mothers take pleasure in raising their children.

I need my children.

All of them.

I am not sure how to get the perfect cultural impartation right because there are instances where I reject cultural notions and think that it is only there to cloud up the mind and restrict people from using common sense.

I also want to share my private opinion about culture as I see it and, in some instances, the lack thereof. I am not persuaded that mock-up exaggerated religious zeal that shows no tolerance to others is of God.

I think it is the very distorted cultural practice that needs to change. I think at best, culture that distorts me reaching out to another is a fraud. I would rather not have it or embrace the desirable cultural practices of another than continue to live in fear so that I can belong.

The next chapter is for the culturally discontented. Do not continue to read if you are not ready to have your blood boil.

Cultural Hybridisation

How long, you simple ones, will you love simplicity? And the scorners delight in their scorning.

(Prov. 1: 22)

Do Afrikaners really have a culture?

What screams culture in my ears, and take me on if you dare, is racism. Surely culture incorporates how you should conduct yourself and what Afrikaners do is teach their kids not to involve themselves with black people. Afrikaners shouldn't be involved with Africans they say, even an insane mind would pick up that something is not right in this saying.

They do eat biltong, are extremely religious, wear the traditional clothes you see at the Voortrekker Monument, eat various traditional foods, and have their own language.

I hear the music and see the unique instruments, and I am convinced that there are sporadic traces of culture here and there, but there is no depth.

Culture is so much more than a trend of oppression. I am not talking for everybody as you do find rotten potatoes in every bunch. Even the best of cultural practices have those disoriented few who decontextualise them and make them null and void.

Culture is not the shoes on our feet. Even without shoes, I take bold steps knowing that I am treading on the soil of our fathers and mothers who laboured on the land tirelessly so that we can enjoy the life's rich tapestry we see today. My Father's land, the land of my Fore Fathers, the land I own but made to be inferior in because of my skin colour.

Even when I could or could not afford shoes, the soles of my feet grounded me. As I walked on the earth in the dust, the colour of the dust touched my skin and reminded me that I am indeed an African.

Africa is not home to the black, white, green, or blue, but all who call it home. It is not a location but a cultural transfusion that is transfused in the very air that we breathe.

That being said, let it be known this day that I am not my culture.

Yes, I use it as an anchor point, and it is my pride. However, I am not my dress code. I am not the garments that I put on my body. Clothes are a mere covering created by mankind to cover the flesh that hosts the inner, real me.

Dare not make this mistake: I am not the colours and clothing on my body. These beads do not dictate who I am. Their sparkles are not a direct correlation of what is going on inside. These beads tell a story that I understand. They make me proud to be an African.

Whether I am dressed in beads, a corporate suit, or not dressed at all. I am who I am. Clothes are not my body. My body is not me, but the perishable part of me. It is merely the part you use to identify me, for now.

I can change my outfit here and there to make you believe that I am another, but my core remains unchanged. I know who I am. I am not a garment or the labels on them.

The colourful homesteads make me smile from the inside. They remind me of my rich heritage and a tapestry of hope that I know exists within me. They remind me of the great footsteps that have treaded on the earth before me. They remind me that I am from a lineage of a culture that I revere.

That being said, I am not my geographical location. I am not confined to a specific location. I am not defined to dwell within the crests of the mountains and walk with my feet on the ground that nourishes me.

I am not limited to a specific location. Even when I am where I have never been, I am home. I am a child of the soil. I do not need to see the blue skies to know that the sun is shining. I do not need to hear the grass brush against the grain.

All that I need and want, I have. I am whole even when I do not feel like it. I am together even when all around me reassures me that I am broken. Right here, right now, as I am, wherever I am, I am whole.

I am not my language.

I do not need to hear the words that I know for them to be more real to me. I am not broken when I am not called by phrases that I knew when I rushed to the river and jumped in with my hands raised in glee.

Even when I am not spoken to, I am not afraid. I am not limited to being addressed or not addressed. I am not the dance that was passed down to me from generation to generation.

I am not the colour of my skin.

I need it and hold it dear. It tells a story. It is part of my identity and I appreciate it so much. It tells of power and strength. It relays a painful encounter that includes the struggles of slavery and the liberation that came with freedom.

I am not my hair.

It reminds me of my roots and reminds me that I am who I am. It is hard to manage and often seems like it has a mind of its own. It can move from a bad hair day to a celebration of something entrenched in my identity.

Liefling is not the colour of his eyes.

They stand out and twirl in the sunlight. They are stunning and alert. Vibrant. Passionate, and true. In as much as I see them, they are not him.

They are a part of him. He does not serve the eyes. The eyes serve him as he dictates that they should.

Liefling is not his traditional food.

I am learning all about his traditional dishes. I try cooking them and often cook the same way that he prefers. Rather than let food divide us, we command food and convert it into that which we want so that it can serve us. It unites us, and we enjoy it.

He is not the songs that he whistles.

The sound of these songs is sweet and fills our ears with great tunes. It is something bound to a heritage of a nation I respect, for they brought me the man that I love.

Another thing that he is not is the biltong (dried meat) that he loves and other traditional delicacies. We embrace them. We hold them dear and value them, but he is not that.

He is not his language.

It is very important to us and goes a long way. It is something that we respect because it matters. That is something intrinsically linked and cherished. However, it is an element, a representation of him. It is not him.

We are not the stares that we get. That is not the culture fostered by a biracial couple. When rejection surfaces, we quickly acknowledge that it is not us. They are not rejecting us but the fear within them. Yes, at times, I am a little concerned, but I know that I am not a slave and that I am free and so I can do as I please as long as it is moral.

I am not my emotions.

The tears of pain and joy that come from these eyes are not me. They showcase the state that I am in. They are like stars that reflect the glorious light of the sun.

All else is just a signifier. It is a sign. A representation. Elements that reflect the whole. They look as though they are the core and one can be excused for thinking so, but this is not the case. Even my vital organs are not my core. They are part of what I use to function. They are avenues. They are not me.

Now that one has a better idea of what I am not, scrap all that out. Even what you think I am needs to be discarded and challenged. I am not who you think I am.

Subdue the drums.

Don't bang them or call for a drum roll, for my identity is not embedded in the noise and screaming declarations but in an almost still profound knowledge deep within me.

I am a spirit, dwelling in a body and having a soul which is linked to my emotions. I am not what my limited mind can fathom. I am made by the Great One and in the image of the Great One.

I am who God says I am, pretty much like who God says you are.

It is not about claiming that religion is a part of any culture. What use is boasting in being a religious people if one cannot accept another race that the same God made and loves? How can we limit God to such an extent that a black woman can't be formed out of a white man's rib?

How can the same God that made all people in his image be made to favour one particular race over another? I am not for a culture or anyone who claims to be dominant by oppressing other people.

I refuse to think that this misrepresentation of love personified is accurate. God is Love. That I know is true. I also know that those who cannot tolerate other races now will *enjoy* eternity when we all share in the same heaven forever and ever.

God is not for one but for all. He is not there for a specific people but all. How can the one who made languages prefer a certain language over another? There is no favouritism in him. Only fools see favouritism in him.

Is there a heaven for blacks and is there a heaven for whites? Is there a separate eternal home for children that come from mixed race relationships? Certainly not! That kind of superficial division would be hell!

Real heaven is a place of unity.

It is where brothers and sisters connect because of love and not physical appearances. It is synonymous with getting along to the extent that others are not just tolerated but truly and deeply loved.

The same blood is the one-and-only in me and you.

The same love that captivates one and draws the hardest vagabond to their knees is the only one that qualifies us all to enter into an eternity of Light. It is Grace that surpasses all human interventions and transcends all man-made traditions and cultures.

In as much as I want to leave a mixed cultural, financial, and emotional legacy for our children, I want to leave behind a legacy of love. I want them to know that they can be anybody. I want them to know that their identity cannot be dictated by mankind.

As they grow up and leave home, I want them to know that they have it in them to have dominion of wherever they are. Ruling is not linked to arrogance, for a real leader is one who serves and gives beyond the call of duty.

I want to leave a heritage of love that will transcend to all people, regardless of how they look or what they have done. Where I leave off, I want these angels to take the baton and run with it.

I don't want them to look back. I don't want them to reverse along the way. Love empowers you to go on. Love picks you up and puts you together. Love alone is the song that we all know even though it is never taught to us.

I want to leave a legacy of love!

Love that knows no boundaries. Love that is not restricted by societal constructions but that breaks barriers to reach out and resuscitate the living. I do not want to be enslaved to tradition if it is meaningless to my cause of love.

Let love alone be the standard. Let love be the benchmark and target. I want to recognise the divinity in you. I do not want to judge you by flaws or the past but to see who you are and appreciate that even more than I appreciate myself. True love serves. It forgives and forgets. It remembers no wrongs.

I want a love that goes beyond the love of the mythical Roman gods.

A love that is able to love with just a glimpse. A love that is able to arise from even the poetic and blunt. I crave to leave a love that will be remembered even after my final breath.

I don't want the love of man-made or imagined idols; I want to know the agape love of the living God.

True love calls out to true love. Love calls out to love and freedom. Love liberates. Hatred draws circles in the sand. Hatred says it is over and leaves. Love returns and embraces even the candidates we so often despise.

Love says, even though we are not alike, I need your blood to keep me alive. I need something in you to restore something in me. Love says, these may not be the hands that broke you, but these same eyes can embrace you. These hands can see you through.

Love says there is nowhere else I would rather be. I am not here because either one of us deserves to be here. I am here because I love you today as I will love you tomorrow.

Even if tomorrow comes and you break today, I will be here to sit with you. We can stay in today until you are ready to permit tomorrow to come.

I am not interested in the divides between us; I am interested in the unity that comes from knowing that we are children of the Great One.

The very love that refused to let me go is the legacy I want to leave behind. The same love that decided to love is the love that I want to impart to my children. It is love that is not easily angered.

It is love that is a lot of things and still knows that it is none other than love. I am not who I think I am. I am a creation intricately crafted by the creator. Just when you think you have me all figured out, I want to die to self.

I want to leave a legacy of love.

I am not talking about the heated-up passions that go on behind closed doors but love that consumes even without a touch. However, if you stick around, I will give you a little snippet of what goes on behind closed doors.

I often get asked these questions by those close to me who are curious.

Pretend you are curious, and I will pretend that I just so happened to feed into your curiosity . . .

A Little Curiosity . . .

There is a way that appears to be right, but in the end it leads to death.

(Prov. 14: 12)

I get asked this a lot. A whole lot of curiosity lies in this chapter. Not just the nosy questions but a little bit of giggles. If this is information overload, I kindly ask you to move to the next chapter.

This chapter is about turning on the lights, when the lights should be off, to illuminate the curiosity that we are often confronted with from those who want to know.

Once again, I must mention that this is just my story. I am in no ways saying it is the story of every interracial couple or that this is how it is for everybody. I guess this is *my* delectable tale.

Lucky me.

We are now going to proceed to a sort of question and answer mode, except that I am going to provide the answers. You can figure out what the question is as you go along.

Let me go for the kill and answer the most asked question. The ultimate hit that gets asked over and over by both men and women who have the urge to know, but don't often like asking . . .

Yes.

That's the answer. You know that question that is in your head round about now, the answer is correct. Now shall we proceed to the next question in your head? Tell me when you are ready.

To those who may have missed what the most popular question was, I will make it even clearer. The question is this: is sex the same with a white man as with a man of another race?

My answer is yes. There is no difference because he is first my lover and then comes his skin pigmentation.

Regardless of his skin complexion, if there is *chemistry*, it will be sustained. If it is not there, whether you are white, black, blue, or orange, you will have a challenge. It is not something that is coined because of your shade.

There are also aspects that have nothing to do with race but the biological composition of a person. This is unique for everybody. You either have it or you don't. I am content, to put it modestly.

If truth be told, size does count! That is all I am going to say with a big smile on my face. I have neither confirmed nor denied why I said this statement, but if you really think about it, you will get what I mean.

One thing that I can say without any hesitation is that white men are generally very romantic. That part I can tell you. It is not a specific person but the general norm. Don't get me wrong, we won't limit it to a specific race, but it is more prevalent.

White guys generally kiss more in public. They hold hands a little more and are more affectionate. They do not just reserve the intimacy for the bedroom but do so continuously throughout the day.

When it comes to general affection, rather than only take things to *parliament* (the bedroom), I see his affection throughout the day. It comes as a kiss on my forehead, randomly holding my hand and stroking it, a gentle embrace, and so forth. Yes, these are small gestures but they have the power to bring a smile in any woman's face.

Affection is not just one major event but a series of little episodes that build up all the time. There is continuous progress, constant affection, and communication. It becomes a lifestyle.

We find ourselves continuously falling in love. Throughout each day, there are little acts of kindness, constant affections, and many touch points that connect us. There are many little things that reassure me that he just thought of me.

The day is filled with reminders that transcend time.

Sometimes it is the song in the car or the lunchbox made with love.

He instinctively calls me to the extent that he would wish to call another but end up calling me. It's almost like second nature. Instant attraction that plays out each moment. Not each and every second but lots of them.

Our kisses are fire. All it takes is a kiss to convert our chambers into a puzzle to be constructed and deconstructed without words. I don't think that it has anything to do with whether he is white or black, but the alignment that we both have when together.

We move in sync. His body paces itself to mine and commands mine to come into line. Other times, it is my music that whispers into his ears and captivates him. He is mine to instruct.

Oh, what pleasure is derived from being the underdog and the one in charge. When it comes to *parliament* (the bedroom), we switch between being the leading lady, to the man in charge, the make-believe audience and whatever else tickles us fancy.

There are no demarcated roles, only pleasure. It is the one point that we can share and know that we are safe. It is something special for just the two of us. A *detox* or an instigator of naughtiness.

Speaking of which, sorry . . . I got to go. Let's just say this is not one of those things I can freely put in my so-called open journal.

Between Life and Love

My son, if you accept my words . . .

(Prov. 2: 1)

'The last time that a white man was here, he kicked the door and was looking for my son.'—These were the words that got to me. They are words from my grandmother when *Liefling* coincidentally met her.

In the words above, she was referring to the *Apartheid* (Segregation) era, when the white soldiers would kick open her door, invade her home, trash down her sanctuary, and search for her son whom they considered to be a terrorist.

These same 'terrorists' were considered to be freedom fighters who sacrificed their lives in the pursuit of freedom. The man that was wanted high and low, who could not even come home to rest without fear of the white government finding and torturing him, was a hero.

I am not going to debate the fine line between hero and foe that existed then, but I can say that I, like my grandmother, am most grateful that today we can sit together at one table.

I recognise that having *Liefling* there reminded my grandmother of a very painful past. Yet I take comfort in the reconciliation of her tone, for she did not speak these words in anger but sincere reflection.

Here was a woman who watched her son being hunted down like a rabbit because he did not want to accept that he was inferior or that it was okay to carry little booklets and be dictated to where you should live and which race you were permitted to befriend.

Today, years later, I find myself in a similar situation. I am being dictated to concerning the depth of relationship that I am having with a white man. I am not only being persecuted but rejected because I have dared to love across the colour divide.

Not only is our door now being kicked, but it is being shut. The punishment is none other than banishment. Solitary confinement when you have beloveds. The beloveds would rather walk away than be associated with a fellow beloved who loves a black woman!

The black woman is a constant reminder of the mindset of a slave that is now dominating their inner chambers. She is also a painful reminder of power that is no more in the hands of the oppressor. The oppressor is not a white or black person but the mindset devoted to segregation, intolerance, and injustice.

When I recall the relatively warm reception that *Liefling* received and the one that I will not receive for fear of being assaulted off the farm, I am reminded that we are still in combat for the transformation of the mind.

We may be theoretically resuscitated, but if both the son and prospective daughter-in-law are not permitted to set foot at the home together or speak about each other for fear that another world war will ignite, on what grounds can we say that we have racially moved on?

In spite of all that has happened in our country, here we are, nothing else matters. It does not matter that we found each other in the weirdest of ways or that just being here together is a profound mystery to be celebrated.

Yet, let us not be deceived; people need people. There are underlying cultural undertones that matter. When one is in a committed relationship, there comes a time that one is introduced to family elders.

To be honest, I do not see this happening in the near future unless there is a miracle. The reason solemnly being that I am black. It would be a direct conflict of interest. Insubordination at its peak.

Having spent so much time in a metropolitan city, one gets so used to the integration and hybridisation that you are almost shocked at feeling shocked over not knowing what to expect.

Let's go back to *Liefling* and my grandmother's encounter . . .

Unlike the last white man that came decades ago, this time the white man was being ushered in. He did not kick the door. He knocked and waited. She could have opened the door to change or shut it in front of him.

This time, he was standing there, saying I know that we are not the same, I know the treatment you received from those who walked in here before me but it is love that joins us. This time, he was there, hoping for acceptance because of the blood that connected us as opposed to our differences.

Here was a guy, in the middle of somewhere and nowhere, outside of his comfort zone, saying I want to know you more. His presence there was courageous. Even without knowing what to expect, he took a step to find out.

It is very easy to assume. It is easy to ignore all that we think we know and all that is, for what is going on in the head. Rather than assume this and that, they met albeit unintentionally. There was a joining. A transferral of realities.

There was a deliberate intervention to share realities and acknowledge the past. It was not about pretending that this is normal but rather stepping out and taking the first step, that being to greet and be greeted back. To exchange greetings.

There they were, two strangers who have never met before, but were willing to try for the sake of moving forward. It was a little awkward at first. It was a little nerve-racking because you didn't know what to expect.

However, as the initial shock dissipates, friendships and experiences are formed. It takes knowledge and the willingness to step up and do that which you never knew you could do.

Before long of what seemed like forever, there was hope. Hope in the sense that there is acceptance. This may not have been the anticipated outcomes, but it was that which it was.

Here was a white man at the door, longing to be himself and embraced into what was none other than foreign ground to him. His presence there was more than enough. The acceptance of his presence was comforting.

Yes, there is still a long way to go, but with acceptance and people longing to step out and be vulnerable, there is hope beyond hope. There is a chance. A spark longing to ignite into a flame that will purify our distorted realities until we are refined by the refiner.

Acceptance is not always a sudden embrace, but accepting that which is now there. It is the willingness to let go of the past in order to forge new relationships. It is saying that I did not expect you to be here, but now that you are here, feel at home.

It is not something that is said, but felt. It transcends words and all that can and cannot be expressed in general phrases. Acceptance says you are divine. You are perfect. You are as you should be. It says to the other that your state is whole, and I accept you.

This reaffirms that your presence here does not take away from me because I know who I am. You being here does not ruffle me up because I am part of an evolving world. Creations changing and adapting reassure me that it is okay to constantly transform and be what I am.

It is not about figuring someone in one breath but acknowledging that they are here because they want to be here. They chose to be here. Their presence is deliberate. It is neither intuitive nor coincidental.

One day, young and old started a conversation. A discussion that continued to resound long after the tyre tracks left. A little hope goes a long way. It moves on even after the beings are gone.

An exchange of words is an exchange of breath. Life itself.

When my presence was announced on the other spectrum, what came to the fore was that 'Sy is swart'—she is black. It is considered normal to get shocked, particularly in areas where racial integration was not common.

It is not that there was a difference or resentment. No, the whites and blacks got along well. There was common ground understanding and clearly demarcated restricted access.

It is when you impress the notion that she is no longer a worker but wants to enter into your sphere as a daughter, share the same blood in your body, have unlimited access, *that* you stir the waters.

Don't for one instant make the mistake of doubting that these are good people. They are just uncomfortable. The idea of having children with the best of both races is not one that was imagined.

It is okay to read about this and hear the story, but when one of your own moves outside of the demarcated boundaries and brings you another who is not what you expected, it's something else.

Shame emerged. A feeling of inadequacy erupted. Is your own no longer good enough? Why? Where do you get this tendency from? Many unspoken fears arise. These are warranted. These should be spoken. It is when these fears are not spoken that the real trouble begins.

Rather than starting a discussion to express feelings of concern and addressing them in a safe and protected manner, nothing is spoken. Nothing is heard. There can be no mediation because there are no discussions. The channels are closed.

This would have been the opportune time to talk about this. It is okay to feel angry and afraid. Rather than shutting down, this was the perfect moment to talk things through and relate life occurrences with each other.

Instead of words, what comes out is fear. Fear expels and rejects all that is not confined to its comfort role. It was a mess. It was a big mess. Few words were spoken and those that came out drew a line in the sand.

It was 'us' and 'them'.

Separately, there could be definite cohesion, but together, there was animosity. When the relationship was cast in stone, and there was a farmer and a labourer, it was different to having a working black woman, who not only has her own home but could now come and call this place 'home'.

Just the thought of a white man willingly choosing a black woman brought instant disdain. It was not the type that was hidden but one as thick as the tangible tension in the room.

I was not there when his beloveds reprimanded him for being with me. In many ways, I am glad that I was not there because it would tear me up to see the one I love stuck between the love of his beloveds simply because he loves a black person.

Love calls out to a higher level that believes the best in all things. Even when cast aside for loving 'interior' people, love corrects us and reassures us that only love alone can transform us to a life of royalty.

Under no circumstances should love be repelled. There was a time that this outside pressure weighed in on us so much so that we separated. It felt better to get away from the drama and pressures.

It was good to no longer worry about not being accepted or being in a state where I wondered if this is right or wrong. I did not give a damn about not being wanted. It felt good to be liberated.

Why was I bothered about people who did not know me and judged me by my colour? Why did I care that they were not willing to waver and wanted to control the lives of others who dared to move beyond this distorted view? A part of me did not care. Another cared because I knew they were important to him.

I care because I love him. I care because I can see that it is eating him up inside. His actions reassure me that he is here. When we worked out the chasm between us and resolved that we will neither protest nor engage in trying to find solutions for the greater good, but would do our part, restoration began.

Regardless of all that we are not permitted to feel, because we are crossing colour lines, we are together. We do feel it. We can't pretend that we never existed or wish ourselves away.

In spite of all the threats and arrows, the reality is he is here with me, and I am very much with him. There is something special about him. A twinkle in his eyes commands my gaze to behold him. He is who he is to me.

I cannot wish him away. I cannot pretend that what I feel is watered down by all that I am specified to feel. There is something that we both cannot deny. It is a soft fondness. A tenderness that comes with knowing someone.

It is generally accepted that people change. People are worthy of second chances and many more. However, when people do not want to change and do not see any errors in their footsteps, then it is something else.

It is not that I want to get along because I fear that I may lose him; he is already here. However, I want to remove the line in the sand and incorporate all beloveds because we are here because of love.

Love says, we may not have started on the right foot, but there is more that keeps us together that what sets us apart. Love says, I may not know you, but if given time and will, we may just be the best of friends.

Love acknowledges victory but says let us all partake. Let us get more people to join. Let us open up the barns of love and invite others. Love says, in the midst of falling rocks and tumbling chaos, 'Here is a crest, come in and find warmth and safety.'

Love acknowledges that we all need each other, that there is something in you that I need to sustain me, and that in me is the intervention your soul may be seeking. Love says let us dine at the same table and drink of the same cup. There is more that bonds us than that which tries so hard to separate us.

I do not reach out for myself, but for the man that I love. I love him enough to let go of my want to be right. I care enough to surrender myself and incorporate fellow beloveds. There is no need to choose. His presence already affirms that one.

Love says that there is no need to choose because love has room for everyone. Together, we are all on the same team. We are on the team of love. Love says, 'Come, there is room for everyone.'

Like the stars, they are plenty, but have a special spot for each one to fit in perfectly. Like children in a playground, there are enough toys for us to share. There is ample room to run around.

Unfortunately, while some see parks and playing children as a source of joy, there are those that use it as a platform to infiltrate the minds of children and convert them into little racists that take after their forms.

In as much as we do not mind having a white and black child play together, it is considered a taboo. What is terrible is when a child is told that it is wrong. The child is told that the problem lies in mixing races.

I have said it before, and I will say it again—leave our children alone!

Playground Integration

A wise son hears his father's instruction . . .

(Prov. 13: 1)

It was very important for our children to know each other and come together. As children, their role was to play and be loved. Children should not be cornered into a reality that leaves them hanging. They should always feel loved and cherished.

From the onset, it is worth mentioning that both our children have survived the trauma of divorce. In as much as one tries to cushion the blows and add some frills, divorce scars children.

They are not in a position to understand. If it is something that alters adults, how much more for children. Knowing this, we did not want to shock the children further, but tried to create transparent and solid acceptance.

We acted after much deliberation and eventually brought them together. At first, the two played together, but one was a little reserved. It was not a forceful immersion, but one that was observed and treated with the greatest of care.

Before long, the children eased up. They were chatting and playing along. Language barriers arose here and there, but all in all, there was effective communication. This was a big step for us and for them.

On the one hand, they were not completely unfamiliar with the concept of such a couple, but on the other hand, it is always different when you get to meet someone that you never knew you would meet.

As they found synergy and fusion, we knew that our relationship was headed to another level. We fused at a level that is higher. We connected without touch.

We were not taking chances any more but were investing in a future together. I appreciate my earthly possessions and so does he; however, it is without a doubt that I can testify that our most valuable and priceless possessions are our children.

Our children come first. Their joys are ours, and their pain gets multiplied within us a hundred fold. They are not only the first place, but the uncontested first. Sharing our union with our children was not just a mishap, but something that was structured and thought about.

It was priceless. Most valuable. There they were playing together. Perhaps the most memorable instance was when we all participated in finding me a puppy. There is something cute and cuddly about little dogs. You melt. Soften up.

The children did just that. With the focus on the puppy and its lovable characteristics, it transcended on to them. It was a great family bonding experience. It was special to all of us.

Both the puppy and all of us were in unknown territory. Like the puppy, we found ourselves in unfamiliar ground and in need of love. We found love, and it instantly felt like home.

There was hope. Great hope. As the puppy wagged its tail in contentment, a sigh settled within us. We were going to be just fine. Here we were as a family. It was not the family that either one of us could have imagined, but it was where we were allowed to be ourselves.

As you are in the moment, you ask yourself tough questions. There are the precautions you take so as to protect them completely. Unlike with your own kid, you have areas you cannot go to.

On the one hand you are a mother and that is the relationship that you have with these precious ones. Mothers protect and have a lot of shock absorbers. However, at the very core, is love.

Mothers love their children. They do not have to be my own for me to love them with the love of self. They are most valuable beloveds. That was a good enough description. I care for them deeply.

We monitored ourselves so as to conduct ourselves in a worthy manner. As adults, we had to lead by example. The tone had to be set by us. We fostered a bridge of communication and an environment that was relaxed. Threats were removed and Peace dwelled in our midst.

I remember being caught in the moment and thinking to myself 'wow', we have come a long way. Even with the craziness going on with the adults, here were the children eating together and playing as one.

To say that it was special does not even come close. It was invaluable. Something that we will not forget. There was nothing out of the ordinary other than parents loving their children and wanting to unite them. They responded positively.

The sleep overtakes the prize.

It occurred at my place. The children were safe and snug. We checked and rechecked. The mood was refreshing. It was one of children being in new territory, but together. Together we took on a new dispensation.

Night descended and day ascended. When the children returned to their normal environments and days passed, we individually went back to get some feedback. In some instances, the feedback got back to us.

He was summoned by his beloveds. They summoned him to come home the next day, if he had the guts to face them after his embarrassing taboo. A text message announcing the disdain at where the kids had been came through. It commanded him to come and see them without delay.

He relayed this story to me.

Unlike when he normally stopped the vehicle and others came to greet him, there was nothing. Silence came. Silence found him. Nothing happened. He broke through the silence and went inside.

There was silence for about ten minutes.

One pretended to look at the television and the other was silent. It was dead silent and uncomfortable. Time passed very slowly. It stopped and then changed its mind and slowly ticked.

During the silence, there was fear. Physical discontentment. Something was broken. Things were not as they used to be. A line that was drawn on the floor had been broken. It did not exist any more.

Silence hovered in their midst. Something was very wrong. There was an ill that needed to be amended. An irrevocable error was committed. The clock decided to tick, but it was the hearts that beat.

Beneath the decent composure was nothing but rage. There was a hurricane ripping apart the inner markers, and it was in full force. The storm blew and destructed the living.

This storm was disguised as silence.

It was hidden behind what looked like composure. Things were not as they looked. The silence did not need to speak; it was shouting. The silence commanded the living bodies to sit still and not move.

Silence fell inside the room as dust and powder. It came down like a blanket that covered people. It froze their bodies. Silence was there to protect fellow beloved.

The silence was broken.

'How much more do you want to put these kids through? They told us where they were.' Those were the longest sentences that were spoken.

Two sentences at a go. They were consumed by decent composure. Silence returned.

Go away silence. Allow my beloveds to speak. Even in my absence, I felt the silence. I knew that something was wrong. We had integrated the children's playgrounds. We had united families.

A man who loved his woman brought his children to her. He was there to monitor the situation. Two people in love merged combined families. In spite of us doing all we could, we could not shield them from the pigments of our skin. That would be like asking someone to be taller or transform the colour of their eyes. It is asking for too much. It is not possible.

Silence found me where I was and confined me. I found myself unable to move. I did not know if I should run or stop or shout. I wanted to drive over and explain that I love this man and would never hurt the children. I wanted to run to myself and meet myself at an intersection within myself. I craved to do something.

The same nothing that kept me up and unable to work was in the very room where he was. He explained. His beloveds expressed relentless disapproval. She was black. This was said to be worse than the embarrassment of his divorce.

His broken marriage was the cause of great embarrassment to his beloveds. It was a shamble. He let them down. Just when one thought he could not disappoint his beloveds more, he did. He fell for a black woman.

Not only did his relationship embarrass them, it was said to have embarrassed the children. It was embarrassment upon embarrassment. Utter silence resided. More was said, but the best way to describe it all is with silence.

The beloveds were silent. The long drive back was consumed by silence. Silence came and knocked. Silence danced in the sky, painted the clouds, and walked on the earth below with silent tracks.

Silence called out to more silence. It knew his name. It slithered in and consumed my name. It tried to come into my work. I hid it and would not let it show that as I worked; I was held hostage by silence.

Silence pinned me up against the wall. It had me broken and sore. It made me feel bad for wanting all my children to come together, even if it was once in a while. Silence wanted to make me feel bad for loving unreservedly with my deeds, words, and core.

Once silence had arrested beloveds, it came and consumed our relationship. We broke up. If silence could be quantified, then one can say there was great silence. Silence of magnified proportions.

Silence brought its partners and took over. It was terrible. The man I adore was no more. He was, but there was a bridge of silence between us that we did not know how to climb over.

How do you climb over silence?

How does one command the silence to go? It was terrible. It was like seeing a swing move because of the wind but not observing any children on it.

Silence swallowed up what could have been and grew with each sigh that replaced what should have been a spoken word.

Silence tore us apart. Silence scrapped into what could have been and consumed it. Love reversed into the beauty of our past and swallowed us up. Silence left no stone unturned. This is where it should have all come crumbling down.

However, in the midst of the silence, just when silence had gained dominion, the impossible happened. Right there, when everything was boxed up and ready to be burned. Just when two individuals who had given up before were giving up again, love returned.

In the midst of the silence, in the presence of unequivocal silence, love showed up. Love found us in our solitary confinement.

Silence had a stronghold and Love knew it. When we were buried deep by silence, love protested. Love stepped in and removed all the lines and boundaries erected by his beloveds. It crashed the silence. It gave us a word. The same words that united us. Empowered with this new knowledge, we took on our fears and boy, did we have fears!

Fears

... For he guards the course of the just and protects the way
of his faithful ones.

(Prov. 2: 8)

I am uncomfortable. What I am about to open up about is not easy to share. It is easy to describe the greatness of others or the majesty of the future. It is easier to say that things are not so, and if they were, they would be great.

A big part of me longs to say what is not. I sort of want to spice up things and remove the sting to dull the arrows and numb the pain. It is never easy to talk about fears. It is easier for me to talk about victories than fears.

On the one hand, I want to lie and say that I have no fears. I want to say that I know exactly what went wrong in my first marriage and have addressed everything to the extent that I am confident that it will never be a problem again.

I want to put on my shaded sunglasses and hide behind them so that I do not have to come clean that I don't have it all together. There are some fears that we have. There are valid fears that I have that I just don't know how to remove . . .

I don't want to isolate him from his other beloveds. It is not that I doubt where his loyalties lie, but the knowledge that I care for him. It

112

hurts me to see him have to choose. I fear that one day his beloveds will walk away from his life and that will be a huge burden on me and our relationship.

He needs his beloveds. The blood within you forms a bond that none other can match. We all need to fall back on our beloveds from time to time. It is another thing when the beloveds are there but do not want to talk to you because they feel that you let them down by loving a woman of another race instead of one of your own.

I fear that we may not get the blessings of our elders. That matters to me because it is how I was raised. I would, however, instantly pick *Liefling* over any culture that segregates against others because of their pigmentation. However, I realise that it is not so much the culture, but the false interpretation thereof.

It is not so much the culture, but it is the people here and there that do not embrace change. The majority of people, just like at church, are open and willing to learn and love.

We do get stares at church, but that is mostly because people are not so used to an interracial couple. It is not the stares that separate, but the looks of those who do not know how to react but are willing to start with a smile to soften the stare.

I am afraid that in the end, based on the deteriorating state of affairs with beloveds, who are very upset at the interracial relationship, that he may be forced to choose. At this rate, there will be no blessings, no communication, and no attendance should we ever wish to take our relationship to the next level.

The man I love will be isolated from his family.

His good name will be tarnished as one who was a rebel, and not a believer, because he loved a black woman. His role as a father will be compromised. That concerns me because I know how much he loves his children and is so proud of them. They are his life.

I fear that in being with me, he will not be judged by all of his actions but will be summarised as one that hated his own people, rejected them, and settled with a black woman.

I have genuine concerns to fear that being with me may affect the quality of relationship that he will have with his children. He is a great father! No one is perfect, but he is a great dad!

He loves his children greatly, and I have the greatest respect for them as a fellow mother. The fact that they are part of the man that I love makes them very special to me. I love them like my own.

I fear that one day I may just wake up fed up with all this madness and personally go *there* to ask how this entire madness can be resolved. In spite of knowing that I will conduct myself with the greatest of respect, I do not know how my presence will be taken.

According to *Liefling*, just me going over there is enough to cause a racket of Biblical proportions. It will most likely not iron things out and open up a mature discussion but lead to something else.

Our combined fear is that while all this drama is going on, our children are watching. Impressionable minds are seeing all this and may start thinking it is okay to expel someone you love because they are in love with a person of a different race.

What effect is all this going to have on the children? Will they think that it is okay to continue to live in silos that do not overlap with others of a different language?

What are our children projecting when adult beloveds are not able to get along and come up with matured solutions that were inspired with international values and principles?

In a day and era when black economic empowerment is predominant in South Africa, can you really afford to be grooming young Afrikaner children who cannot tolerate the sight of blacks? Is this hate not career limiting?

I fear that we are growing vipers. They are children, but we are busy tearing apart their humanity. We have no right to fill children with struggles that erupt from adult discontentment issues.

I fear that we are grooming racists. I fear that all this may just get too much and one of us could just pack up and leave. I fear that I do not fear at all because even when I am afraid, I will strive to do it being afraid.

I fear that we may be so concerned about transmitting culture in the form of languages, food preferences, and customs but miss the real culture that actually matters.

I fear that we are so focussed on the culture that you can see to the extent that we may forget all that goes on inside. We may be so busy decorating the outside to the extent that we forget that it is the inner man that counts.

I fear that I am not sure how to heal the rejection that we subdue these children to when we confuse them with our petty arguments. We constantly send them mixed messages and then get shocked when they are a little confused.

They are confused because they see black and white living together at ease on television depictions but are met with disdain and fear when it actually does happen in real life.

We have thought of relocating, but I am not going anywhere. There is still life left in me. There is a fight that emerges from a woman deeply in love, ready to stand up to protect her family.

I am ready to stand even when it feels like there is no more fight left in me. I stand up and command my bones to regroup because I do not want my daughter to live this way. I want her to be free to love and see the beauty in others.

I am doing this for my baby. I am doing this for generations yet unborn so that they can love most purely without fear of being sequestrated. Let the conversation continue. May it proceed.

I don't want our children to live this way. I don't want them to feel apologetic for opening up themselves to another who is willing to be there.

Although I have all these fears, I do not fear sitting down and having a mature conversation with foes. People who undermine God, those who can't see beyond themselves.

Conclusion

Sight

Pay attention to your teacher and learn all you can

(Prov. 23: 12)

Let us go through the mountain in pursuit of moving to into the future. Let's take on a dispensation that we cannot sort out at this point in time and take it forward. The generation before me had racial tensions. They struggled to get along. Lovers who were from different races were arrested or exiled.

Today, as a new-generation lover in love with someone pale, we are threatened to be disowned. Fellow beloveds cannot force us to depart or be exiled and so they remove themselves as a way to control us.

They isolate themselves so that we are stuck in solitary confinement. They remove themselves as an undisputed form of protest. This is still a taboo. Love *out there* is okay, but love that lapses pigments is not welcome in a personal way.

Come, let us climb the mountain because the reality is that all this is happening in what should be a new South Africa. It is new, but the mannerisms are still old. The rainbow has not fused. The colours are still separate and orderly set apart.

As we approach this mountain, let us see without sockets and embrace without hands. Let us dare to depart from this very instance to hold on to the hope of what we will see and experience at the top of this mountain.

Now that we are at the top of this mountain, let us take in the air. Let us open up to breathe from a higher altitude. May we adjust to the different angles and acknowledge all that our new reality brings us.

Love found me. Like a lot of other single career women, I was looking. I was just clicking away, hoping that someone the other side of the screen would be there at the right time, sitting and thinking about me.

I was hoping that of all the things that could happen and not happen, regardless of the time differences and flopped experiences, what if the one that my soul sought after could be sitting down at the very same moment in time, reading the same message, not distracted, and engaged with the quest of finding me?

Here I was sitting behind closed doors. I was all closed in. What if love could somehow penetrate through these walls and signal some flickers of hope.

Love remembered me. Before I knew it, there we were, talking about God. Suddenly, here I was coming to the understanding that maybe, just maybe, this is not a typical conversation with a random person.

Yet something in him spoke to me to the extent that a greeting, turned into a courtesy greeting, being returned and then a conversation and eventually a meeting.

It was not planned. I hoped that it would happen but was not sure that it could. I did not even know how to love him. He was different and yet we spoke the same love language. There was more that brought us together than all that separated us.

I did not know him. He was a stranger to me, and so I spoke with the stranger. The stranger knew my name, and I got his. We were no longer strangers. A simple hello had broken down the geographical divides.

Little did I know that in loving, I would be hated to the extent of wanting to flee from my own country. I could not have guessed that in opening up my soul to him, I was opening a can of worms that would spill open a lonely set of occurrences.

My intention was to get to know him a little more. Speak to the guy on the other side of the screen. Get to know his name. What followed next was not part of the plan.

It was the part that you dream of. What if, right now, in a location undisclosed to you, was someone who would come into your space and take away the loneliness?

What if it were possible that in spite of the various odds, love could nudge another to turn on their screen, make that call, or bump into you as you take the corner?

What if, as you were reading, your soulmate was reading this same page, pondered on this same spot, read the same sentence again, and thought of you? Regardless of whether you have met or not, what if you were the object of their desire and crossed their mind right about now?

Dream no more. Dreams do come true. Yet along with dreams come the will power to defend your dreams. Along with aspirations come the need to fend for that which you believe is distinctly yours!

In falling for the white man, I fell for a nation that still had unresolved racial disputes. In loving him, I saw a line of disdain and hate get drawn and crossed and drawn again in the sand.

Sometimes it got so bad, we wanted to run away and leave it all behind. We thought of running away to another country and continent where people were treasured for who they are and not because of the colours of their entwined hands.

I want to love him and all that is dear to him. I choose to love him and his beloveds because love has convicted me that it knows no boundaries and does not reside in specific people.

I am convinced that love is an element that allows people to have first, second, and third chances. Even with all the strokes and hope ruled out, love says continue. When counted out, love does not stop.

I am not advocating for, or against, multiracial relationships. I am simply calling for love to be given a platform.

I want to love him with one more breath and with the other and the other. When there is nothing left, allow me to love in the sphere of eternity. I am one persuaded by love.

I stand as a soldier of love, ready to take orders. I am armed with bullets of patience that come from love. Kindness emanates in the place of discontentment. Joy pours over and nourishes the me that I now am.

When banished and feeling like a foreigner in my own skin, I don't run away. Long suffering is part of the innate strategy deployed. Rather than hate, I seek out the good in others and pray that one day, I will be counted as a human being.

I am just an ordinary woman that is deeply in love. Someone just doing her thing and doing it to the best of her ability. This is not my first attempt at love but one that is worth exploring.

Love allows me to not envy those who are not faced with the same challenges. I celebrate with them and understand that everyone is engaged in some sort of battle. I respect where they are and celebrate the ground that they have covered.

When I am downtrodden, it feels like it is easier to pack up and count my losses than to wage against racism that filters down and affects me in my very own private chambers . . . I stand.

Sometimes, I stand even though I am afraid that it is going to tear us apart. There are times that I stand solid with unadulterated conviction.

I resemble a rock, a crystal that is hard and persuaded. A rock that does not powder.

Then there are those moments when I am consumed with thoughts of what the future holds. But then I gather myself and remember the me that I know thrives within my chambers. Even in the midst of trembling.

The mother within me gives birth to soldiers of love. I am fertile. I multiply. Even when I look like I have taken a fatal blow, I replicate.

It is love alone that enables one to truly have dominion. It is only through love that I can reach out a hand to those that don't love me to say that I am not the unimaginable horror that I am esteemed to be because of the colour of my skin.

Love allows me to not only turn my other cheek, but it awakens a song in me that I can only sing when in the heart of overwhelming pain. Rather than detonate, I sing.

I sang to fear when it tried to lower my status and classify me as less than adequate because I am black. I sang to statements that are of a derogatory nature and hummed when our inner man was disregarded.

When he comes home and is full of pain from being insulted for loving one less worthy because she is black, I do not want him to choose. I see him come back. I see the door open, and he walks through the door.

Even without saying a word, I know whom he has chosen.

He takes the blow like a general. There are some comments and attacks that he does not even reveal to me. He dims the pain with his arms. He does not do so to conceal but to try and protect me to the best of his ability.

In reaching out, I am trying to educate. Yes, there are language differences here and there. One often turns to resort to their mother tongue at the weirdest of times. It is not that one does not know better but more of a reflex action.

I am allowed to be me and He is allowed to be himself.

It is not so much about changing who one is but loving who the person is. Allowing one to be human. Allowing one space to falter and be accepted with shortfalls, weaknesses, and strengths.

There are times when I allow him to get away with murder. Not in the literal sense, but with things that don't sit so well with me. I refuse to sweat over the minors and overlook them because even though they are not my preferences, I appreciate the totality of him.

Our taste in music may not be the same, but we both appreciate music. In spite of the lyrics and tunes sung in the shower, the pitches may differ, the voices may not be in sync, but the love of music and making songs is there.

My desire is that he will be true to himself. As he is, I love him. Even though he is at war with his own, I know that love really does change everything.

If I could change one thing, I would remove the minors from the front row seat. I would excuse them from having premiere seats of an ongoing racial battle between adults. It is not our stable and solid relationship that tears them apart; it is the disdain they are constantly witnessing.

It is not okay to put ultimatums and encourage the splitting of two people who are just trying to be there for one another simply because he is white and she is black. It is not okay to think that if their union ever resulted in children, those children would be freaks and outcasts instead of the best of both worlds.

I want all our children to play together as children do. It is not brainwashing and indoctrination that I seek, but to simply have them eat ice cream and play in the sand as children do.

When one is not feeling well, may they see that they are brothers and sisters and that a hug transcends all language barriers. A smile is an international language. A gentle embrace goes longer than many words.

I am still asking myself the same question though: is he the one?

Do I know like I know that he is the one that all of me is utterly convicted about? Is he the one that enables me to walk through fire and not burn because I know I have to live to see his smile just one more time?

Sometimes the answers are right in front of you. That which we seek is not a concept that is out there or a pie in the sky. It is within our very presence.

I know that I would rather have him here with me even though it is easier to let him go and go after our designated 'own kind'. I know that as a career executive, I would not allow anyone to address me in the way that I am addressed by his beloveds; and yet I still reach out.

I come as I am with nothing up my sleeves. I raise my arms and reveal that there is nothing hidden in my hands. I open up. Even after opening up, open up some more in an effort to be transparent.

When I am in his arms and he is in mine, it all comes together. We make sense. All else falls apart. As our hands entwine, there is no space between them. He holds me, and I hold him back.

The glimpse does not speak. It does not provide solutions. It does not overlook that not only do we have racial challenges but are also faced with the wonders of integrating families and mixed children. The glimpse does not ignore our ages or that at times it just gets too much.

The glimpse simply acknowledges that if ever you have doubts, just know that my presence here tells you all you need to know. When the door opens and I step in, I chose you all over again. I don't need to tell you; just know that my presence here is all you need to know in order to *know*.

I acknowledge the glimpse with a delicate gaze. In the gaze, I say thank you. In the gaze, I smile. I know that as I gaze back, he knows that I am here. Here I am gazing at the man with whom I endure it all. The gaze simply says I know your name.

That's all that matters. In silence, we know profound mysteries that voices cannot utter. It is going to be okay. No matter what comes, I won't regret taking things to the next level and making the time to meet in person. I won't ever regret falling in love.

www.ingramcontent.com/pod-product-compliance
Lightning Source LLC
Chambersburg PA
CBHW051439280526
45785CB00003B/1357